D1108272

Date Due

THE
DISCIPLINE OF LETTERS

THE
DISCIPLINE OF LETTERS

BY

GEORGE GORDON

OXFORD
AT THE CLARENDON PRESS
1946

OXFORD UNIVERSITY PRESS
AMEN HOUSE, E.C. 4
London Edinburgh Glasgow New York
Toronto Melbourne Cape Town Bombay
Calcutta Madras
GEOFFREY CUMBERLEGE
PUBLISHER TO THE UNIVERSITY

DISCARDED-LIBRARY
HUMBOLDT STATE UNIV.

PR
99
G54

PRINTED IN GREAT BRITAIN

PREFACE

'I'll make a bunker in the sands of Time,
And write a book with chapters ere I die.'

THE gay challenge to fate was flung lightheartedly
by George Gordon in an hour of informal talk
with his early pupils. Throughout his life his books
with chapters were always in his mind: he planned
them, gathered his material, and on occasion wrote a
passage. They were to come to life in later years of
leisure. One of these, *Shakespearian Comedy*, skilfully
edited by Sir Edmund Chambers, was published in
1944, two years after his death. Many others—*Johnson
on Milton*, *The Language of Shakespeare*, and the rest—
lie in embryo among his note-books, a treasury of
reflections and bibliography.

The curiosity of his mind, always open to a new
venture in literature or scholarship, the boundless
diversity of his interests, and the increase in his ad-
ministrative duties, all united to frustrate his plans for
his *œuvres de longue haleine*. He was, therefore, led to
express himself in essays and papers written under the
spur of some special occasion. It is idle to regret his
unfinished work, since what is left shows well enough
the quality of his mind at work, his craftsmanship, and
the range of his scholarship.

Of those essays and papers this volume contains
a selection. He revised all of them during his last
illness except his final lecture from the Chair of Poetry,
Gerard Manley Hopkins and Robert Bridges. It was
delivered in 1938, shortly before his descent into 'the
tunnel of University administration'. 'Could a novel
be written about me', he said at the time, 'the appropriate title would be *Professor into Mole*.'

The last essay in the volume is a tribute to the
memory of J. S. Phillimore of whom George Gordon

was in his undergraduate years at Glasgow University an affectionate and admiring disciple. It was delivered as a lecture in 1937, and polished to his liking in the last few weeks of his life.

I am much indebted to the Delegates of the Clarendon Press who have approved the essays chosen for this volume: also to Sir Humphrey Milford, to the Secretary of the Delegates, Mr. Kenneth Sisam, and his colleague, Mr. D. M. Davin, for their advice and help in the selection.

MARY GORDON.

June 1946.

CONTENTS

I
THE DISCIPLINE OF LETTERS[1]

IT is an ancient practice of Universities that a new Professor should voluntarily come forward and at once exhibit and explain himself. The subject of his discourse may be anything he pleases within the area committed to him, but as a rule, I imagine, what is desired on such occasions is some statement of the lecturer's beliefs: his faith in the studies which he professes, and his ambitions for their future. He is expected to do what can never be easy: to justify as a scholar the use which he makes of his time, and as a teacher the tax which he is empowered and is probably determined to levy upon the time of others. It seemed impossible to refuse so honest a challenge; and you will observe that, if I wished to avoid it, the subject which I have chosen allows me no escape. If there is any heart and soundness in the matter it should be there, in this Discipline of Letters, this *Disciplina Literaria* which I proclaim.

The Merton Chair of English Literature, to which I have had the honour to be appointed, was occupied from its foundation until his death a year ago[2] by one man. It is a short history, in this place of long successions, but I doubt if in the annals of any University, in the history of any Chair, there are to be found eighteen more brilliant and creative years. I was an undergraduate when Professor Raleigh came, and in temporary exile from these studies, but even to the junior *penetralia* of *Literae Humaniores* the news came through that English Literature in Oxford had at last

---

[1] Inaugural lecture as Merton Professor of English Literature: delivered before the University of Oxford, 9 May 1923.

[2] Walter Raleigh died on 13 May 1922.

procured its man. It had taken seventeen years to be allowed to find him. Time passed, and by what I must always regard as the happiest accident of my life, I found myself, in the kindly magnificence of Magdalen, a member of the same society, and generously admitted to more than a beginner's share in the growing fortunes of the School. The older humanities of Oxford, forgetting their heavenly flight, were at that time something of an Athenian neighbour to the new studies: it had been thought that one knew English, and could read Milton when one liked. But these were the dregs of the Renaissance. It is now generally allowed that a language and a literature with a history of some 1,200 years, not devoid either of masterpieces or of worthies, are possibly deserving of the best scholarly attention which the country can afford, and that the disadvantage under which they seemed to labour of being our own language and our own literature, and not the language and the literature of some other country, has in all probability been exaggerated. Raleigh, in those years, lived for his School, and though sometimes anxious and sometimes indignant, was never seriously troubled about its future. He feared in the end that he had been possibly too successful, and that in the popularity of the School something of its austerity and fitness might be lost.

It was a royal beginning for a very ignorant young man to learn his trade from Walter Raleigh. I saw how things were made, and how even the hard material of institutions can answer to the play of mind. I was taught, not dogmatically, which was never his way, but by figure, in a thousand tossing similes, that Literature is in fact a partnership, and consists of Men and Books; and that, in spite of all appearances to the contrary, men are usually more important and a good deal more interesting than the vehicles they drive. I am probably not the only person in Oxford who first learned from him what a College does not necessarily teach—the meaning of a University, and why some arts and not others are called liberal.

It is hard to say from a rostrum what should be said about Walter Raleigh; for though no one adorned it more, or, I think, more valued its privileges, since it allowed him to address the young, he was happiest where men are equal—in rooms where no one lectures, on roads where all men walk, in air which all men freely breathe. I must not attempt to add to the many portraits which his friends have drawn of this singularly lovable man of genius. I am addressing an audience which knew him. I will speak only for a moment, and it shall be of his teaching and his professional opinions.

Both as a teacher and as a critic he was undogmatic, knowing well that for every dogmatist life is waiting somewhere and will catch him in the end. His lectures, and particularly the conversational teaching in which he excelled, were in this respect like his familiar talk: they were experimental, rich in afterthoughts, and full of incidents and of surprises even to himself. It was felt, as the theme warmed, that anything might happen, and the expectancy of his audience was shared by their instructor. He was never harsh, and though he disliked the dogmas of his trade, he did not as a rule attack them. He was content to describe them, and when the description was finished it was usually found that attack would be unnecessary.

He was acutely aware that the academic study of English literature has not been uniformly happy. Much of the academic criticism of his time seemed to him to fall into the absurdity of the famous art critic 'who, lecturing on the Venus of Milo, devoted the last and briefest of his lectures to the shape of that noble work of art'. But he did not despair of his fraternity, nor lose confidence in its manhood because of the unlovely adolescence which it was his mission to relieve.

There are signs already of a better time, when a maturer scholarship shall make amends to life, when, even in literary treatises, a smile shall play about the lips of truth, and learning, having digested (preferably in concealment) the accumulations of a century, shall be once more polite.

I have never known a man who, if it were presented to him, more quickly recognized a piece of clean and independent work. For Research, on the other hand, as commonly understood in the Regulations of Universities, his regard was more distant, and the word did not readily pass his lips. We have all learned to be wary of the arts by which young men and women, under laborious instructors, only succeed at last in being dull in a new way. 'The welfare of mankind is not much promoted by bad dissertations on good books.' To all men who have discovered truth Research is known to be only a compendious and (as it has been used) a somewhat pretentious name for the very natural process of finding the answer to a question, and to be valuable in proportion as the question seems worth asking, and is, or has become, the spontaneous interrogation of the student's mind. The thing must be unforced: not wrung, as Milton says of schoolboys' essays, 'like blood out of the nose'. 'You cannot hound a man into writing a good book.' Walter Raleigh preferred the older way, and was of that company of the critics and historians of literature whose work is itself a part of the literature which it celebrates. He believed that in that broader track—and indeed in all—no School of English Studies, if it were alive to its opportunities, was better qualified to lead than the School of English in the University of Oxford. 'We cannot afford', he wrote eleven years ago, 'we cannot afford to have a weak School in Oxford; and all that we dare to hope of the best that we can build is that it shall not disgrace her name.' He would state it as almost a law of nature that no man is allowed both to build and to inhabit. He lived, however, to see his work assured, and the School of English which he had planned and moulded number itself without apology among the humanities of Oxford. He looked forward to a time, not necessarily remote, when the Oxford School, with the Clarendon Press behind it and the Bodleian at its elbow, should be the headquarters of English Studies for the English-speaking world.

In any University at almost any time there will generally be found some dominating study or discipline, whether elevated to importance by a tradition of great teachers, or by the simple pressure of demand. At one time it is Law, at another Philosophy; in one place it is the Classics, in another the Mathematics; but whatever it may be, this dominant study absorbs the rays of authority, and keeps the sun off the rest. Oxford in common repute is pre-eminently the home of classical studies, of that admirable discipline which embraces in one view the languages and literatures, the history, philosophy, and art of classical antiquity—of what, until the other day, we could still call, without misunderstanding, the ancient world. It is a just, but it is a modern pre-eminence, and has more of the marks of Victoria upon it than of the Georges or Queen Anne. The mathematical author of *Hints to Freshmen* spoke no doubt for Cambridge alone when he informed his clients a century ago that 'it is a good custom to set aside a part of the afternoon for *literae humaniores*'. But Waterland's advice, *alma Anna regnante*, to devote the mornings and the evenings to Philosophy, and the afternoons to the Classics 'as requiring less coolness', was good advice at Oxford for a century. In this scramble of the arts, this battle for the golden hours, English Literature took, at that time, no public share, but lay in wait, like all seducers, for idle moments: for those hours of vacancy which educationists have fortunately never understood, because, as a rule, the secret of them dies with youth. It was in obedience to no precept that Mr. Shenstone and his friends two centuries ago met 'almost every evening, the whole summer' in each others' chambers at Pembroke, where they 'read plays and poetry, *Spectators* or *Tatlers*, and other works of easy digestion, and sipped Florence wine'. It is a nice question for an academy what we are to call this—work or play. I should never dare to answer. Dr. Johnson has asserted, indeed, that Mr. Shenstone '*employed* himself at Oxford in the study of English poetry'; but *employed*, we are informed by a member of the party, was not the right word. It should have been *amused*. Mr. Shenstone, it appears, '*employed* himself in the study of the mathematics, logic, natural and moral philosophy, and the other sciences usually taught in a University; he made (we are assured) a considerable progress in them, and was fond of them'. Let Mr. Richard Graves be right. Employed or amused, Mr. Shenstone left Oxford with a considerable knowledge of English poetry, which the University of that day had no means of rewarding, with some insight into gardens, and without a degree. I have known people to be offended by that common way of thinking, of which Mr. Graves was guilty, which classes English literature with the amusements and the relaxations of life. But I could never understand the quarrel, nor spend a moment's indignation on the statesmen, the great lawyers, or the captains of industry who *unbend* their minds over our English poets. I can think of no prettier original for the classes of our English School than Mr. Shenstone's parties, nor, I believe, would any member of those classes desire an origin more formal or abstruse. For let us work as we may (and we work hard), let us steel ourselves with industry, we are still, by a vagrancy of blood, like all the arts of enjoyment, members of that first house of the humanities whose children were begotten upon Idleness by Love.—Dr. Johnson amused himself with Chemistry.

In Oxford to-day these things are better understood, and the age of studious dominations is over. The fences are down, and the ancient gardens or enclosures of learning are now indistinguishable, except by the number and the ability of their cultivators, from the other and newer portions of the field of knowledge. I am conscious of a general goodwill and liberality to studies other than one's own which always, indeed, distinguished the good periods of this place, but is now much more widely and more handsomely diffused. I can think of no better name for it than that old one of Humanism: a free and companionable interest in all generous knowledge, whatever its object, whether in the works of Nature or the works of Man. The Classical Renaissance, which rebuilt our Schools, and in the end enfranchised the modern literatures of Europe, began by degrading them because they used the vulgar speech. It depressed English literature for two generations, and English literary scholarship for three centuries. If I were to sketch a portrait of the spirit of this movement it should be a figure of great majesty and severity, carrying in its right hand the elixir of life, but in the left a vial of scorn, of which, in our day, the last contents have been spilt. I am inclined to believe that the varied interests of life, the genuine concerns of men, are better represented in Oxford at this moment, and that the balance of our studies is more equitable and unforced, than at any time in the seven centuries of our history.

There is a story in Hogg's *Life of Shelley* of a certain Paduan Professor who made a tour of the principal seats of learning in Europe. He came to Oxford for some weeks, and conversed with the leading persons, and what impressed him most were these two very remarkable peculiarities, neither of which he had ever

met with in any other University. The first was this.
Wherever he went it had been his practice to inquire—
'Whom do you consider the first man among you in
learning and talent? Who is the second? And who
is the third?' In every other University he had received a prompt and decided answer; here and there,
perhaps, some difference of opinion might occur which
name should rank as *third*; but as to the first and
second, unhesitating unanimity. At Oxford, on the
contrary, and at Oxford only, nobody would ever tell
him who stood first. 'In what way? In what walk of
science? In what department? In what branch of
knowledge?' 'Pray tell me, who is the first among you
in *any* way?' There was no answer.

The second peculiarity was this, and it made the first
more striking. At every other mart of learning, when
a point of knowledge came up, he had often heard the
answer, 'I do not know', but at Oxford never.

It is an interesting tale, and may even be true. The
foible of omniscience still lingers, but as an eccentricity
of individuals. The republican equality which even
then distinguished Oxford among the Universities of
Europe has been extended in our own day from its
teachers to its studies. There are no peerages in the
commonwealth of learning. The Discipline of Letters
is republican.

An attempt has indeed been made to disturb, or at
any rate to ruffle this equality in favour of the studies
which I represent. It has been claimed, with much
force and very much more eloquence, by one of those
Departmental Committees which came in with the
Peace, that the English language and literature should
occupy in the education of this country, and occupy at
once, that position of ascendancy which the Classics
are believed to have resigned; that in all our schools, if
not also in our Universities, this study, since we are

Englishmen, should have precedence over others. For plainly, whatever our pursuits, we must all speak English: why not, therefore, speak it well? We all write English: and how uncommonly badly we do it! And there are few of us who do not sometimes read English literature, with that degree of understanding which is permitted to men whose humanities were founded on the Latin grammar. The Report of this Committee[1] has had a sale which novelists might envy. It has been highly and sometimes justly praised. It is a work of goodwill, and is therefore welcome. It has good things in it. But it advances a view of literature, and especially of English literature, which has scarcely received the critical attention it deserves, and a view of English scholarship which fortunately has been less respected. The Professor of Poetry[2] to whom scholarship is not a luxury but a mode of life, has removed the book from his shelves, and reported his relief. His successor in London,[3] speaking at necessarily greater length, has been equally emphatic in condemning a publication which proposes that students of the English language and literature should omit at will the first six centuries of their history. I share the views, on this matter, of both these gentlemen, and their not unreasonable hope that University Schools of English will continue the good practice of beginning at the beginning. But Universities are unlikely to be more than entertained by proposals which assume that undergraduates cease to read when they are presented with degrees, and that the student of *Beowulf* and the *Anglo-Saxon Chronicle* may be heartlessly defrauded by never reaching Keats. In this University Mercury and Philology, after many deeds of settlement (for the lady has been difficult), are partners, I hope, for life. The literary doctrine must be worth examining

[1] *The Teaching of English in England* (H.M. Stationery Office), 1921.
[2] W. P. Ker.   [3] Prof. R. W. Chambers.

which on its higher or University branches bears such very poor fruit. It is briefly this: that England is sick, and that English Literature must save it. The Churches (as I understand) having failed, and social remedies being slow, English Literature has now a triple function: still, I suppose, to delight and instruct us, but also, and above all, to save our souls and heal the State. For this end everything must be hastened; there must be short cuts and quick returns; *Beowulf* must go if Burke may not be 'mastered'. Literature, to these reformers, is everywhere a sacrament, a holy remedy, and apparently almost the only sacrament now left. We are warned, with splendid disregard of human history, that the nation of which a considerable number rejects this literature, or, as it is called, 'this means of grace', 'must assuredly be heading for disaster'. Sir Walter Raleigh once defined great literature as that body of books which had been found useful in circumstances never contemplated by their authors; but he could not have foreseen such a test as this. I doubt if Matthew Arnold himself, with whose feathers this Report is plumed, would have undertaken to reassign, in an English literature of sacrament and panacea, the very different places which must henceforth be occupied in public estimation by Chaucer and Shakespeare, Dryden and Johnson, Fielding and Lamb.

The place of Universities in this mission, and more especially of their Schools of English, is vividly described. They are 'the apex of the educational edifice', and in another passage they are 'the inner shrine'. Professors of English Literature may therefore be regarded in two capacities, either as steeplejacks or as priests. But they must also be actors, since literature lives in the drama of the spoken word; organizers, because multitudes who have not 'heard whether there be any Holy Ghost' are waiting for them, or for their 'missionaries', beyond these walls; propagandists, because the multitudes must be coaxed, or they will not come, though a moment ago they were waiting; teachers also, 'of the teachers of the great English-speaking democracies'—and to the students now flocking to them for research their responsibilities are also heavy; the ambassadors, lastly, of the New Poet, who shall come, like another Laon, to save a world in which Government and Christianity have failed.

'The time cannot be far distant when the poet, who "follows wheresoever he can find an atmosphere of sensation in which to move his wings", will invade this vast new territory, and so once more bring sanctification and joy into the sphere of common life. It is not in man to hasten this consummation. The wind bloweth where it listeth. . . . The interim, we feel, belongs chiefly to the Professors of English Literature.'

These, then, are the new requirements. I confess myself unequal to them, and doubtful if Nature can ever be expected to provide, in a single organism, so rich and incongruous an assemblage of qualities. It is hard to refuse one's friends; and the writers of this Report are friends of literature. But perhaps no great harm will be done. For these, I am persuaded, are not the rumblings of a new age. They are the slack drums of the Victorian era.

Meanwhile the working-man stands solid in his darkness, distrusting literature, we are told, and clubbing it with the antimacassars of 'middle-class culture'. He is much in the thoughts of this Committee, who approach his case with the circumspection of an early bishop winning barbarians to the Church. I have the greatest sympathy with him, and there are even occasions when I see his point. The working-man is not wholly in the dark. He perceives, and is not alone in perceiving, that society has other forms of expression than literature, and forms not less noble; that the place of literature in the world has natural and salutary limits which are not to be extended by exaggeration. There are times when the coolness of Mark Pattison is welcome. 'Cultivation commensurate with the range of the human intellect', he reminds us, is not to be given by means of literature, nor is that nation to be wholly congratulated in which literature and the arts are 'the highest intellectual objects'. I observe, and not only in this Report, the growth of a religious jargon about literature and literary genius, and I observe it with regret as an affront to life. We must be modest to be believed.

'If there are qualities in literature which are above price these are also to be found in the world of manufacture and finance—in that huge pyramid of loyalty which is modern industry, and that vast network of fidelity which is modern commerce. Yet iron-founders and cotton-brokers do not, in discussing the operations of their profoundly beneficent trades, express themselves wholly in terms of genius and virtue.'[1]

I suppose it is apparent that I am no great admirer of the English Report. *Et tamen habet admiratores. Habeat . . . sed Londinienses.*

Here in Oxford we have plenty to do without saving the State. We have a large and growing School upon our hands, and among our projects one considerable reform, in which we shall march, I hope, with every School of Letters in the University. Our 236 undergraduates present a problem more impressive by its size than by its complexity. As the School matures they find themselves progressively more comfortable. They are reasonably cared for, and care that is more than reasonable was never very good for undergraduates, nor by the best of them much welcomed. Their immediate seniors, the young graduates of this and many other Universities, who come to us for training, are less enviably situated. They have outgrown our friendly makeshift of supervision; what almost did for ten will never do for seventy. It is generally agreed that some-

[1] *Johnson on Shakespeare*, p. xiii (O.U.P. 1915).

thing must be done. We can no longer support by acquiescence a system which invites young men and women to advance knowledge, and having brought them from the ends of the earth, bids them good-day at the door of the Bodleian. They expect to be welcomed (though our Regulations, in fact, make no such suggestion), and are surprised at the well-founded embarrassment of their reception. In the end they forgive Oxford, as capricious beauties are forgiven; but they remain uninstructed, and we remain uninformed. There are things which even the born scholar, when he is young, needs to be shown, if for no other reason than to save him time: and what time means to a scholar is a story too bitter for this occasion. The cry of Casaubon rings through the centuries: always 'Time, Time, more Time!' The scholar's mirage has been described by Wyttenbach in a passage which Mark Pattison, because he also knew this mirage, has translated:

'From the vantage ground of my youth I looked down over the outspread stretch of life on which I was entering, as upon a limitless plain. The task I had set myself (an edition of Plutarch) seemed to be close before me, and within my grasp. But as age advanced, things assumed a different aspect. The horizon of my span of life drew near, the horizon of my task receded. Ten years passed away; the end of my labour was not even in sight. Five years more; and what remained to do was still more than what had been completed.'

Even laymen can understand the rapture of Laplace when he speaks of John Napier, whose logarithmic tables had 'doubled the lives of astronomers by reducing the labour of months to days'. We can save these young men time, and advance the day when scholars shall less often than in the past become the life-long drudges of their own youth, laboriously executing by methods acquired in middle age the schemes hit off in their careless prime.

It is a great question just how we are to do it. I think that we shall be equal to the problem, and that the time is ripe. We cannot much longer expect the Clarendon Press to train, and to train on proof-sheets, half the editors of England. It has been hitherto our only training school, and no better could be looked for than a School with such masters as the late and present Secretaries, and which enrolled such assessors as Sir Walter Raleigh and Mr. Nichol Smith. I hope that our relations may still be intimate, while we relieve it of some drudgery and some expense. I shall always be proud to have made my second graduation in the Secretary's Room, and to have received the friendship, and sometimes the approbation, of Charles Cannan.

Whatever we do I hope that we shall avoid the common error of belittling our past and importing salvation from abroad. We have been indolent in this country, but we have not been idle. Our scholars have not organized, but they have sometimes thought. Our record is not inglorious though our constitution is unwritten. It is a discovery periodically made, and characteristically by ourselves, that England lacks seriousness, and is short of what are called 'ideas'. Carlyle announced it in the forties, in many octaves. Matthew Arnold lay awake in the sixties, thinking of it. Lord Haldane, in our own time, has begged us to get more. The ideas have their fashions, and change with the age. Sometimes it is our literature that is at fault, and sometimes our industries, sometimes it is our science and sometimes our schools. I forget what ideas we lack at the present moment which are to be found in astonishing and shameful abundance in some other country. But if ideas should be granted to us, we lack system. It is true; and we are hoping to do better. In almost all our University studies we are still 'a country unprovided with seminars'. This also

is true, and we are meaning to have classes. We do
wonderful things, but we do not, apparently, organize
the secret. We produce great men who train no
disciples. Our greatest scholars have a strange reluctance to found schools. These, I confess, are not very
good reasons for failing to train our graduates, but they
are worth consideration because they are English
reasons. Most of the English scholars whom I have
known, whether they admitted it or not, have been
suspicious of method, and not very ready to discuss it.
They had their own way of working, and were willing
to suppose that other men had theirs. There is something of the poet and the solitary in our Englishmen
which makes them trust and value most that part of
their work which method cannot quite explain, the
part that comes to them. University seminars of the
standard pattern cannot easily be made of this instinc-
tive stuff. The reaping machine is not seen at its best
when the harvest is poetry. Our scholars, like our
writers, have a way of being intensely national, and
some caution is required before we change them. The
'provincialities' of this country which Matthew Arnold
deplored have been seen by closer students to be in
fact the English character. His recipes for getting rid
of them are better described as flaying: and Swift
reminds us what that means—you would scarcely
believe how much it alters a person for the worse. But
we need not be alarmed. Whatever advances we may
make in system, there will always be room for the
whimsical Englishman and the older methods. No
progress in the organization and machinery of research
can ever supersede the single inquirer and the lonely
work of the mind.

I doubt if any other country has produced so many
unprofessional scholars, of so much devotion and of so
high a quality. That want of system is not to be despised which breeds Gibbons and Malones. They have

been our compensation: we could not otherwise have gone on. The supply, though variable, is not exhausted. Some of you may recall the amazement of learned foreigners, the regular officers of research, as they surveyed the merely volunteer activities of Dr. Frederick Furnivall, that fine Englishman and Commissary-General of the English Studies of his time, doing the work of half a dozen seminars without ever having seen one, leaning on his desk in the British Museum, sitting in his favourite A.B.C., or walking in the street. 'Of gentlemanly manners', says Professor Brandl, 'and without a trace of pedantry, he was yet a scholar of wide range of vision, and an excellent example of those strong personalities which in England make up for the national lack of adequate system.' We have been greatly served by our privateers. I would name, also, *honoris causa*, Henry Bradshaw, Cambridge librarian, and first bibliographer of his own or perhaps of any age, the founder of that modern science of bibliography which is now transforming English scholarship, and of which the most exciting adventures are at this moment being played out, with many hurrahs and some dropped catches, on the text of Shakespeare. This Henry Bradshaw had also never seen a seminar, and what was more (though this I hardly expect to be believed), did not know German. But when Mommsen came over in 1885 to consult the Cambridge manuscripts of Gildas, of all the men that he met in England it was Bradshaw who impressed him most. The recognition was mutual. It was 'as good as a month's holiday' to Bradshaw to see Mommsen getting to work upon the manuscripts.

It is an instructive picture, and may teach us self-respect. The War, which broke so many things, cannot be considered as wholly malignant in its consequences if it should prove to have broken our servility to the lower forms of German scholarship, that nightmare of organized boredom by which all grace and simplicity and nature were frightened from our studies. I think we had ourselves to blame. If the Germans were tyrannous, our scholars were servile, standing, like those Athenians on Sphacteria, τῇ γνώμῃ δεδουλωμένοι ὡς ἐπὶ Λακεδαιμονίους. There is a secret propensity in nature which impels the dunces of one country to admire the dunces of another, and third-rate scholars throve everywhere on a system which rewarded industry and extravagance at the expense of every other quality. If this plague should come again, I recommend the method of Dick Steele, which he learned at Merton:

'I remember, in my youth [he says], it was a humour at the University, when a fellow pretended to be more eloquent than ordinary, and had formed to himself a plot to gain all our admiration, or triumph over us with an argument, to either of which he had no manner of call; I say, in either of these cases, it was the humour to shut one eye.'

There is a Unity as well as a Discipline of Letters: a unity of history and a unity of craft. The modern literatures of Europe are a community through which Greece and Rome have passed. I value the neighbour-hood in this place of the ancient and classical, and the modern and vernacular traditions, and hope that litera-ture and scholarship may gain by it. The unity of the craft of letters is an affair of the household rather than of history, and operates in depth from grammarian to poet. Grammarians or critics, lexicographers or editors, or *vates sacri*, they are all 'of that ilk', and if they vex one another, as they often do, it is a fault of temper. The Poet Laureate writing poems, and Dr. Bridges in-quiring into the nature of our speech, are seen on this view to be the same person working in the same material. In the Middle Ages this was understood. 'The builders of the crypts', says Mr. Ker, 'were recognized and honoured by the masters of the pinnacles; the poets in their greatest freedom of invention were loyal to the grammarians and moralists, the historians and lexicographers upon whose work they built.' In this University, and in this School of English, we stand for the loyalty and the discipline of the House.

There are two things which Oxford, like Dr. Johnson, can do very well. One is, to state, of any literary undertaking, what it should contain, and how it should be executed in the most perfect manner. The other is, to show why, from various causes, the execution has not been equal to what was promised. I have usurped, in this lecture, the first of these capacities of the University, and with less remorse, because I now go to join the martyrs to the second.

II

VIRGIL IN ENGLISH POETRY[1]

A MORE than Virgilian diffidence steals over me as I
stand here, one of the many who in various parts
of the world, and in words well or ill chosen, offer on
this famous birthday national sacrifice at the altar of
The Poet. My theme is noble but daunting; millennial
in its range, and demanding the utmost nicety in even
the briefest handling of it. I must stride like a giant
and tread like a cat. Yet, whatever its difficulties, I am
glad to have been chosen for a task which has revived
old pleasures, and has sent me wandering, with the
Virgilian numbers in my head, about my shelves among
the English poets. The theme unites, as no other could,
the literary pieties of my life and schooling, as of the lives
and schooling, I imagine, of most whom I address here.

That this should be a Warton lecture is evidently an
added propriety, for few subjects can be conceived
more after Tom Warton's heart. The originals of
Spenser, perhaps Virgil's most precocious pupil in this
country, were the topic of his first critical publication.
His edition of Milton, Virgil's greatest English scholar,
was one of his last occupations. And a principal achievement of his *History of English Poetry*, if the tumbled
riches of that still invaluable medley may be so simply
characterized, is to have disclosed in one view the
Gothic and the classical origins of our literature, with
a perfectly friendly understanding of both, and to have
made it easier, therefore, to see in the *Aeneid* not only
the greatest of the Roman classics and the epic model
of the Renaissance schools, but a prime fountain-head
of European romance. The thought of Warton brings

[1] The Warton Lecture on English Poetry, 1931. Reprinted from
the *Proceedings of the British Academy*.

inevitably another to my mind, his successor in these
studies of Epic and Romance, and the first lecturer on
this foundation. Had W. P. Ker been alive to-day, my
place would not be here. I should be listening to him
and learning from him as of old.

I suppose there has hardly been a time since the
Roman settlement when Virgil has not been read or
his name heard at least in this island. We need not
wait for Gildas to quote the *Aeneid* in the sixth century. If Martial, in the first century, could boast that
he was read in Britain, we cannot doubt that Virgil,
the acknowledged prince and saint of Roman song, was
read there also. There were sound Virgilians among
our conquerors, and grammarians in their train, nor
can I believe that the Emperor Hadrian, of whom a
picture remains to us quoting the sixth book of the
Aeneid as he paced his Roman garden, left Virgil un-
cited, or omitted his custom of consulting the *sortes
Virgilianae*, during his visit here. Between that already
established rite and the consultation by our own King
Charles I of the same traditional oracle in the Bodleian
lie fifteen centuries of infinite change and turmoil,
through which, in the Western world, the humane and
mystical spirit of Virgil, that gentle troubled majesty,
stood hardly shaken (on the verge, indeed, in England,
of still new triumphs), having survived with scarcely
a stain the adoration of the schools, the superstitions of
legend, the licence of romancers, and the suspicions of
the Church.

It may be safely asserted that no single poet has
exercised over the poetic production of this country
so long and so continuous a control as Virgil. From
Aldhelm to Bridges is the bluntest statement of its
range. Behind it lies the schoolroom, and those texts
of 'Tityre tu' and 'Arma virumque' which are doubtless
at this moment receiving fresh inkstains, and had their
grubby first baptism more than nineteen hundred

years ago. In the schooling of our Middle Ages and
Renaissance alike, and indeed until the last century,
when Homer on one hand and Shakespeare on the other
upset perspectives, Virgil continued to be for verse,
and for some other things as well, the prime author.
While Latin was still the language of Europe he was
imitated in Latin. When the vernacular took precedence he was imitated in both. For more than four
centuries, that is to say, of the modern world, Virgil
has led, in the metrical performances of his students,
and in this country above all others, a double or
bilingual life. Most of our English poets who have
practised Virgilianism have practised it twice over, in
Virgil's language and their own, with interactions and
effects of intimacy more easily experienced than expressed. If the Roman temper, which meets us in
almost everything that Virgil wrote, has sometimes
seemed to us an English thing; if in our poets, and to
the eye of fancy, our English fields, and woods, and
waters appear at times to be coloured with a more than
northern grace, and to be warmed by the light of some
kinder genius, we owe these illusions, if illusions they
be, more than to any other cause, to our national worship of the Virgilian Muse, and to the tradition which
for so long made Virgil the familiar and ennobling
companion of the English gentleman.

This native and English Virgilianism, which I take
to be more particularly my subject, comes naturally
somewhat late in our history. I spoke of Aldhelm.
But the Latin hexameters of Aldhelm and Bede, as of
their numerous Latinizing successors, are a part rather
of European than of English culture. From Aldhelm,
with the *Georgics* beside him, versifying on Bees, from
Bede meditating,

Arboris umbriferae moestus sub tegmine solus,

there is no great distance, though thirteen centuries

divide them, to the young collegian now engaged on
a similar task of humanism, and looking anxiously (if an
Etonian) for some chance of bringing in the word
susurrus. Now and again some copy of this classical
Latin verse touches native things. Alcuin, for example,
a Virgilian from youth, so that he even feared the charm
of that 'luxuriosa facundia', writes, in the style of the
Virgilian pastoral dialogue, a debate between the
seasons which has links of sentiment with Anglo-Saxon
poetry, and throws a greeting over the centuries to
Chaucer's *Parlement of Foules* and to one of our earliest
recorded English songs. Shall the Cuckoo come? is the
question, and the jury of shepherds say yes.

> Et veniat cuculus, pastorum dulcis amicus . . .
> Omnia te expectant, pelagus tellusque polusque,
> Salve dulce decus, cuculus, per saecula salve!

We can almost catch the gusto of

> Sumer is i-cumen in.

But such things are rare.

In our earliest English vernacular, not yet equipped
for such a guest, Virgil is hardly to be found. Virgilian
properties are there, but not the owner nor his workmanship. Unless, indeed, those scholars are justified
who detect in our otherwise northern epic of *Beowulf*
suspicious marks of Roman structure. There would be
nothing incredible in this, but it so grieves my primitive friends to have it mentioned that I make no claim,
Virgil being otherwise so well commissioned. He was
plundered for the Trojan story and the tragedy of Dido
throughout the Middle Ages, at first, at fifth, at tenth
hand. Set pieces were torn from him: storm scenes,
in which his excellence was early noted, or such tiresome but influential portraits as that of Rumour (Lady
Fame), which was a gift to medieval allegory and made
the round of literature. Aldhelm has it, and Chaucer;
Jonson did not disdain it, nor Milton; until it fetches

up at last and very properly in *Hudibras*. All this went on. But of the essentials of a true Virgilianism, of Virgil's art and ethic, of Virgil's purpose or his personality, no medieval Englishman, not even Chaucer, our first Dante scholar and Virgilian translator, seems to have had any grasp.

> Glory and honour, Virgil Mantuan,
> Be to thy name! and I shal, as I can,
> Folow thy lantern, as thou gost biforn . . .

So Chaucer, setting out, in middle age, to epitomize the *Aeneid*, which he has just read hurriedly through for the first time. But Virgil is still seen far off as one of the Great Men of Old, like Solomon or Aristotle, and a mist of legend surrounds his features and his fame. The parting command of Statius to his *Thebaid* may be taken as statutory in medieval England:

> Nec tu divinam Aeneida tempta,
> Sed longe sequere et vestigia semper adora.

The epic of Rome was in fact surrendered to Venus, and absorbed in the ocean of Romance.

That the story of Dido should take wings and leave the epic temple was no doubt inevitable, and an unconscious criticism of Virgil's art. That story had always popularly so detached itself, even in Imperial Rome. The eyes of the general world have ever turned on the unintended heroine, and left the hero to slink off to his unregarded epic ends. Chaucer is of the popular mind and is staunch for Dido, placing her in the calendar of martyred heroines, among Cupid's saints.

> Anoon her herte hath pitee of his wo,
> And, with that pitee, lov com in also.

Who can resist it, thus put? Or reckon the wet eyes? The story of Dido has haunted the imagination of Europe, drawing tears from saints and sinners, from St. Augustine in the fourth century as from Anatole

France in the twentieth. Thus great literature moves
to its unlooked-for and sometimes unwelcome triumphs.
To that scrutiny of a woman's heart which immor-
talizes the fourth *Aeneid*, to that passion of love which
in his Roman and epic character he does not hesitate
to call corrupt, the creator of Dido owes his place
among the most potent of the ministers of Epic's
dissolute and enchanting sister, Romance. This Roman
poetry of the loyal heroine, says Ker, taught Europe
the eloquence of love, and Dido has had her share in
creating the manners and the sentiment of chivalry.
I would ask you to reflect on the universality of Virgil:
patronus alike of medieval chivalry and Renaissance
humanism, and still the unspoiled companion of our
country thoughts.

Dido went on to later triumphs, and spoke her heart
out on the Elizabethan as on the Roman stage. But,
indeed, the whole story of the *Aeneid* throve there.

> Then he unlockt the Horse; and suddenly
> From out his entrails, Neoptolemus,
> Setting his spear upon the ground, leapt forth,
> And after him a thousand Grecians more,
> In whose stern faces shin'd the quenchless fire
> That after burnt the pride of Asia.

Marlowe, you say; and Marlowe it is, in his *Tragedy of
Dido*, vamping. Now hear him translate, for, like most
of his quality, he knew Virgil. It is the passage in the
first Book where Aeneas meets his mother:

> An Phoebi soror? an Nympharum sanguinis una?
> Sis felix, nostrumque leves, quaecumque, laborem . . .
> But whether thou the Sun's bright sister be,
> Or one of chaste Diana's fellow nymphs,
> Live happy in the height of all content,
> And lighten our extremes with this one boon,
> As to instruct us under what good heaven
> We breathe as now.

How sweetly this comes off! And leaves the distinguished army of Virgilian translators panting! It is the idiom of Shakespeare, of *Comus*, and all finest Elizabethan things. Hear it again—not in translation this time—and calculate at your peril how many years on the benches of a grammar school were necessary to enable Shakespeare to produce a sketch like this:

> In such a night
> Stood Dido with a willow in her hand
> Upon the wild sea-banks, and waft her love
> To come again to Carthage.

Grammar schools and Universities have little to do with such a vision. It is the whole story of the Fourth *Aeneid*, already a national possession, reflected in the cunning mirror of romance.

I have come to think that the most important event in the modern history of Virgilianism was the selection of Virgil's life by the humanists of the Renaissance as the model of what a poet's life should be. It so happens, though this had been lost in the medieval haze, that of Virgil's poetic life more details have come down to us, at any rate more significant details, than of the life and poetical practice of almost any other ancient poet, and from what they reveal two things stand out: that Virgil was regarded, and regarded himself, as in the fullest sense a poet by vocation, and that everything was done that power and friendship could do to let him plan his life, to make the poetical life not only possible for him, but inviting. Of all the Romans Virgil is most definitely the professional, the dedicated poet, and nothing was omitted that might keep him so. Rome had been waiting for such a man, to match the Roman genius with the Greek, and to nurture him, when found, became a duty.

Imagine, now, the situation of Renaissance Europe. As that wind of the spirit travelled north, every nation that felt its force looked about, as Rome had done, with an air of rivalry and expectation, for its heroic

poet, and the question was freely asked how such a man
is grown. The answer to this question of poetical
eugenics was presently agreed to be the life of Virgil,
of the perfect poet, that is to say, functioning as nearly
as possible in perfect conditions. His life was studied
and generalized. The *Aeneid*, in spite of Homer, was
still the working pattern for epic. To that pattern
was now added, from the example of its author, the
plan of the higher poetic life. Poetry on this plane
was declared a sacred calling, and it was taken as mere
fact that an epic poet, one who aims at the highest
and most sustained performance, must plan his life and
education to that end from his youth up.

The new code was briskly set out in the third decade
of the sixteenth century by an Italian humanist, the
'immortal Vida', celebrated alike by Spenser, Milton,
and by Pope. The future epic poet, he lays down,
carefully selected and early segregated, should grow to
manhood remote from cities, among pleasing solitudes.
Lighter pieces may then engage his art, as a diversion
from severer studies: 'prentice things, like pastorals
and elegies. No *Aeneids* to begin with; Virgil found
that out when Apollo pinched his ear. Time enough
for *Aeneids*; let him follow Virgil and do his *Eclogues*
and his *Georgics* first. Presently the young man will
travel; and then—and then—the choice of the epic
subject. But still no hurry; no fear of being late. Virgil
never hurried. Besides, the preparations of an epic
poet must be comprehensive, for an epic poem is liker
a long voyage than anything else. Once launched on
that wide ocean you cannot trust to petty landfalls,
to ports of call, and lighthouse men; you must lay in
supplies before you sail. . . . And, of course, in planning
the epic, you will see the advantage of sending your
Hero down to Hell; you will have Games, and Ban-
quets, and Stories; and you won't forget the Storm and
the Volcano.

This humanist picture of the poetic life, drawn early by Vida, elaborated by numerous successors, and by me, for the moment, somewhat brutally foreshortened, had effects of the utmost importance on our poetical tradition. It determined in many particulars the apprenticeship of Spenser and of Milton, as of many another English poet less gifted and strong-willed, and it directed, almost ritually, much of their poetic procedure. It may be found still active, whether submitted to or not, in Dryden and in Pope, and in its general bearing, in much that it implied of poetic scholarship and self-discipline, of Virgilian quietness, seclusion, and *praeparatio poetica*, it may be detected still working, in varying degrees, in some of the greatest poets of last century: in Coleridge, who abused Virgil, but could not, for all that, get off his shadow (there are *Virgiliana* in the *Ancient Mariner*); in Wordsworth, who translated Virgil, and was denounced by Coleridge for doing so; most patently in Tennyson, the folds of whose admirable mantle were studied in the Virgilian mirror, and whose life was in many ways a Virgilian modernism. The groundwork of the whole is knowledge, and a universal scholarship. When Gabriel Harvey tells us that his friend, Mr. Spenser, 'though not entirely unacquainted with the sphere and the astrolabe, is ashamed of his lack of skill in canons, tables, and instruments', he tells us something that Virgil and Milton would have understood. The author of the *Faerie Queene* was to that extent less well equipped for poetry. In Virgil's profound and comprehensive studies, of which the full extent and accuracy are only beginning to be revealed; in his devotion to the honour of poetry, which his name had saved through the darkest hours of the Middle Ages; in his role of patriot, as the 'new poet' of his day who conquered, by steady artistry, a stubborn language and a reluctant metre; even in his studious reluctance to publish, as 'not fearing to be late', lies much of the high professional inspiration which sustained the authors of such achievements as the *Faerie Queene* and *Paradise Lost.*

The more positive Virgilian debts of Spenser and of Milton are past counting. Echoes of the Virgilian diction, the Virgilian music, haunt their air, and have haunted English poetry ever since:

> And now the sun had stretched out all the hills.
> If thou beest he—but Oh how fall'n! how changed
> From him. . . .
>
> Like to an almond tree ymounted hye
> On top of green Selinis all alone.

The Virgilian pastoral, that frail and impossible beauty, so foolish in foolish hands, but capable of such elegance, such tenderness and capricious grace, we owe in its English forms to that conspiracy of the Renaissance, in which Spenser and Milton were leaders, for importing and endenizening all poetical fine things. There are more massive debts. When we enter the epic world of Milton we walk everywhere among Virgilian structures, and I am of those who hear, as Dryden heard, and Wordsworth, and Tennyson, and Bridges, beneath the grand Miltonic harmony the surge and sway of the Virgilian hexameter.

Spenser and Milton brought home the secrets of Virgil; it only remained to make him an English poet. I spoke of Dryden, and no sounder or more loyal Virgilian ever lived. His style warms at Virgil's name as at no other but Shakespeare's; all his life he proclaimed him proudly his foreign master; and nothing would do but that in the end of his days he must translate him. In no country, I suppose, in the last four centuries has Virgil been so steadily translated as in England. Yet the task, as all have found, is of heart-rending difficulty. 'What Virgil says of the Sybil's prophecies', groans Dryden, 'may be as properly applied to every word of his; they must be read in order as they lie; the least breath discomposes them, and something of their divinity is lost.' Yet he persisted, encouraged by such general and friendly expectation as no translator in England had ever before enjoyed. It provides some indication of Virgil's place in the mind of Dryden's England that, his intentions once known, the nation considered its honour as engaged. One friend presented him with all the editions of his author. Addison wrote a preface, and Chetwode a Life. The translation was composed on a round of English country houses. The first *Georgic* and twelfth *Aeneid* he translated at Denham Court, he tells us, and the seventh *Aeneid* at Burleigh, 'the magnificent abode of the Earl of Exeter'. The hopes of his abettors were not disappointed. Dryden, as Johnson remarked, is not one of the 'gentle bosoms', and much of the delicacy and *desiderium* of Virgil escapes him. But his translation remains by almost general consent what Lord Bowen, a rival translator, has called it: 'the noblest and most masculine of all the versions.' Though 'the silver trumpet has disappeared, a manly strain is breathed through bronze'. Dryden's Virgil became at once a substantive part of English literature, one of the greater English poems, and Virgil entered the eighteenth century an English citizen.

Certainly, in that century, no naturalized author, unless it be Horace, is more at home in England. Every one who can translates him and takes mottoes from him; every Miscellany contains him; he may be tracked from Addison's noble hymn to Cowper's *Task*; he is the parole of gentlemen in every assembly, thundered in the Senate and riposted across the dinner-table. He even enters by right of family, and of that mellow playfulness which Horace noted in him, the peculiarly eighteenth-century field of high satire and mock heroic, giving at times a new fineness and even beauty to its

wit. Every year announced its Georgic and its hundred
Pastorals. Of these eighteenth-century Georgics, of the
Sugar-Canes, and *Hop-Gardens*, and *Arts of Preserving
Health*, much fun has been made, and they certainly
do not shine in the forehead of English poetry. But
I doubt if Virgil would have despised them. He would
have thought that their motive, if not their poetry,
might save them. Virgil's splendid praise of Italy is
in the minds of all their authors, and something of
that patriot fervour, a love of England and the English
soil, breathes in their uninspiring lines.

If I were asked where Virgil, in the eighteenth century, might be seen at his best, I should say in Thomson
and in Burke, for his genius penetrates even English
prose. Thomson's letters are filled with thoughts of
Virgil, and there is no better Virgilian exercise than
to read the *Seasons*, as Thomson wrote them, with the
Georgics by one's side. The style of Burke, who loved
Virgil as Fox did, and whose tattered Delphin copy
never left him, has been described by Hazlitt as 'forked
and playful like the lightning'. Something of that
lightning and of that elemental playfulness he would
have rejoiced to see traced, as I have pleased myself
by tracing it, to Virgil.

We are still, I suppose, though less and less in Virgilian scholarship, under the influence of the nineteenth
century about Virgil generally. That century saw fit
to lose its head over Greek, and to this blameless and
exacting passion must undoubtedly be attributed much
that is best and most beautiful in the thought and
poetry of those times. It was deemed necessary, however, in the supposed interests of Homer and Theo-
critus and the established worship of 'originality', to
deride Virgil, and that is a mistake from which we are
only now recovering. The bitterest contempt for
Virgil's powers, both in epic and in pastoral, came
from Germany. I will not read here, as I had once

intended, the comic effronteries of Teuffel and his
tribe, because they are based on an evident inability
to see that whatever cultures he may exploit, and
whatever devices he may borrow, Virgil is engaged in
the unusual exercise of artistic creation: that he is
making, from old materials, new forms of art. The
Rhine is a boundary in many controversies, and, I am
glad to think, in this. The French have always been
staunch for Virgil, and may still, I believe, when his
genius is outraged or traduced, rely on the traditional
Virgilianism of England. German scholarship in this
matter has gone a long way of late towards reparation
and even repentance, and will doubtless go further. A
professoriate which is now engaged in swallowing
whole that personality of Homer which it spent a
century in disproving may yet regale us by swallowing,
with equal thoroughness and discipline, its misguided
and deplorable abuse of Virgil.

Our poets, on the whole, seem not to have been much
affected by these misconceptions of the really ancient
discovery that Virgil lacked the Homeric *élan* and fell
short of Theocritean naturalism. They had never supposed that these *were* Virgilian qualities: Virgil had
other powers. They continued, as before, to read him,
and to indulge in the national exercise of translating
him; though they turn to other and widely different
sources he is never banished from their minds. Throughout the nineteenth century, in all sorts of places in our
poetry, and in a thousand spoken and unspoken ways,
Virgil was still a presence and a power. Wordsworth
knew him, translated and imitated him, and there are
passages in *The Prelude* which might entitle their
author to be called the profoundest Virgilian of the
century. Keats translated the *Aeneid* while still a
schoolboy, and in *Lamia* and *Hyperion* is sometimes
rewarded for that feat. Shelley had discovered for
himself that Virgilian delicacy of expression which 'as

a mist of light conceals from us the intense and ex-
ceeding truth of his conceptions of Nature'. Echoes
of the derided *Eclogues* are to be found in some of his
finest work, and the tenth has no ignominious share in
the scheme and splendid close of *Adonais*. Landor is
an inconstant friend of Virgil, but of his intimates.
Of his later disciples among our poets the most brilliant,
unquestionably, are Tennyson and Matthew Arnold.
Arnold knew, no man in his century better,

> the Virgilian cry,
> The sense of tears in mortal things,

and speculated on that 'supremity' of elegance which
fascinates in Virgil, and 'makes one return to his poems
again and again'. The position of command, however,
as the most felicitous of all anthologists in this field, has
been assigned to Tennyson, and is no more than his
Virgilian devotion and his astounding art deserve. If
no Birthday Ode to the great Mantovano, 'landscape-
lover, lord of language', has issued from the studies
of our English poets to-day, we know by what masterpiece of salutation they have been deterred.

Of Virgil and the modern world I should wish to say,
first, that by the professional students of his work he
has never, I believe, been better understood. I am glad
to think that in the remarkable revival of Virgilian
study which has distinguished the present century, if
the biography of the poet is more indebted to foreign
scholars, and above all (let me be just) to the scholars
of Germany, the elucidation of the *Aeneid* owes most
to England. Not the least of our benefactors in that
field is in our company now, I mean Dr. Mackail, whose
literary edition of the *Aeneid*, timed for these festivities,
promises to sum up and refine the interpretations of
an epoch.

How much literary popularity the works of Virgil
now enjoy, in a world which has so little Latin and so

much less Greek, I cannot tell. The strictly national
achievement of Milton, his contribution to the poetic
capital of his country, is evidently acquiring, however,
as Matthew Arnold foresaw, a new value. If one
cannot read both Virgil and Milton, it is a great good
fortune to have at any rate the Englishman. But I hope
that direct access to Virgil, so peculiarly an author 'of
the Centre', will not be further narrowed, nor the
highroad of European poetry, of which he commands
the very entrance, allowed to fall to grass. Among
poets, and Englishmen generally who can read him,
he must recover, I believe, much of the favour he may
have lost. There is a new interest in the art of poetry,
in poetic experiment and technique, and, where that
interest exists, Virgilianism can never be far off.

The ordinary Englishman is slow to think of poetry
as an Art, or as anything, indeed, but a Gift, and a Gift
from Nowhere. For a long time, in this country,
Inspiration rather than Training had been insisted
on, what *comes* to the poet, he can't or won't tell how,
rather than his skill and instrumental mastery. As
Bridges puts it, addressing the god of our idolatry:

> Lo, Shakespeare, since thy time nature is loth
> To yield to art her fair supremacy.

Yet the history of European poetry is avowedly the
history of an Art, of a great game played with rules,
nor is the inspiration of Milton more manifest than his
strict and lifelong attention to the canons of his profession. There was the same difficulty in Virgil's Rome.
Horace, in his *Ars Poetica*, hardly dares to speak of
Genius, for, if he had emphasized it, his Romans would
have stopped work. So he speaks all the time of Art.
It is difficult to get a practical people, like the Romans
or the English, to take trouble in the Arts beyond a
certain point, or even to admit that beyond a certain
point trouble should be taken. Why train, if you have

Genius? And if you haven't Genius, what are you doing there at all? We can understand (and so could the Romans) training for Parliament, for a race, for the Bar. But Poetry! One had been given to understand that poetry was spontaneous. For it is not to be supposed that a man of commanding ability would seriously take to poetry if he might be swaying senates, moving juries, or governing a province. He is a poet, obviously, because he cannot help it; which brings us back to spontaneity again. It is, or was, felt that the thing is somehow spoiled if you work at it. It should grow like a flower, fly like a bird, blow like the wind. Training, for a poet, seemed like sending Burns to a university, or birds to an Air School, or Joan of Arc to the military academy of St. Cyr. It is all very absurd, and I welcome the signs of a change of view, of a new attitude which may restore to its natural position in the world of poets the Virgilian art, an art so pure that, like Light, it is a criticism of everything it touches.

III

THE TROJANS IN BRITAIN[1]

IT was a childish grievance among us, when I was
a boy, that our British histories began with Julius
Caesar; and the grievance persisted when we were no
longer boys. Such a wealth of time had passed before
the Roman came: was Britain to be counted voiceless
all this while? no message? no traditions? Empires
had risen and declined; numerous poets had died in
poverty; in a hundred different and even contradictory
ways philosophers had demonstrated that pleasure is
really pain; the world had gone through a great part
of its normal course, it was old and was beginning to
feel it, when Caesar landed and wrote down his remarks.
Was it not a little annoying that Britain should be
dumb all this while, and speak first to the world in
Caesar's Latin?

These are elaborations, the embroideries of an old
grudge. This schoolboy patriotism, as I remember,
was never gratified. We were not even told that it had
not always been so, that our grievance was modern.
I must think it an opportunity lost. For, in fact, this
dumbness, this British silence is recent: not much more
than some two or three hundred years old. The modern
schoolboy is in the habit of envying his remoter predecessors who lived when there was so much less history
to learn, and he has all men's sympathy. But there is
a rough justice even in our studies. The English
schoolboy or undergraduate three centuries ago began
his British history not with Julius Caesar and that
trumpeting date of 55 B.C., but with Brute and his
Britons 1100 years before Christ. A whole Empire
was added to his history of which the modern boy
knows next to nothing, and he construed his Virgil and

[1] Revised and reprinted from *Essays and Studies*, vol. ix.

his Latin Homer with an interest peculiar to himself, for, as he was well aware, the first Britons were Trojans, and their leader, King Brute, was a member of the House of Priam, a kinsman of Aeneas, and an ancestor, therefore, of all the Caesars. Nowadays, when a Prince of Wales sits down to learn the history of his family, he is popularly supposed to begin with Cerdic the Saxon. The little Edwards and Henries of the fifteenth and sixteenth centuries began, we know, with Brutus the Trojan. We have the school books still in which they read.

It was about the beginning of the seventeenth century, in the days when Camden, Speed, and Selden sat in judgement on antiquity, that the shadows of suspicion first began to fall heavily on these British Trojans, after they had enjoyed an almost undimmed reputation for nearly 500 years. They staggered on, still finding defenders, for another half century, persisting still in the popular histories and the popular mind, and flourishing mightily in Wales, but passing more and more, like all lost causes, into the keeping of the poets. The poets had always been friends with them, and it was in the works of a poet that they made perhaps their last signal and historical utterance, in that History of Britain which Milton wrote during the Civil War and Commonwealth. In the new generation of Pepys and Sir William Temple they gradually disappeared from the pages of history, as a fabulous, discredited, and poetical people.[1] The gap which they left remained a gap for many years. The historians tried to fill it with Pytheas of Marseilles and Julius

[1] Interesting evidence of this change is supplied by the earliest *Oxford Almanacks*. In the first (1674) Brute heads the list of the Kings of Britain. Of the 1675 issue no copy is now known, but Brute has disappeared from the *Almanack* of 1676 and the regnal list begins with William the Conqueror. This last is in itself remarkable, if only because the *Almanack* is a University publication, and Oxford was still maintaining that King Alfred was its founder.

Caesar, but fill as they might they had little success.
The hole was too big, and the prehistoric wind kept
coming through. Despairing of texts, they began to
look about them. They dug; they tapped; they tried
Stonehenge. But as every one thought differently
about that impressive structure, they were thrown
back once more. In the end the really notable discovery
was made that digging is an art, and from that time
things have mended. Archaeology has swept up antiquarianism, and carried it to the point where inquisi-
tiveness becomes inquiry, and curiosity almost begins
to look like science. Archaeology now rules in the place
of Brutus and his Trojans, to the notorious advance-
ment, as I gratefully admit, of historical truth, but, as
it has been managed, to the perpetual and inexcusable
disadvantage of all boys, all lovers of old stories, and
all readers of English literature.

> Those old credulities, to nature dear,
> Shall they no longer bloom upon the stock
> Of History, stript naked as a rock? . . .

It was a great day for Science, but a bad day for Greek
poetry, when Zeus got his leave, as Aristophanes tells
us, and Rotation reigned in his place. I confess to
something of the same regret when I think of Brute
and Archaeology: two good things, and both of them
romantic, which after the first drubbings and expostula-
tions need never have clashed. The servants of Legiti-
macy would incur, I believe, no charge of treason if
they extended even now, through their subordinate
dispensers of text-books, a modest and belated pension
to the fantastic household of the old Trojan Pretender.

The Trojans are first heard of in Britain in a late
eighth-century writer, one Nennius,[1] a British priest

[1] *Historia Brittonum*, ed. Mommsen (Mon. Germ. Hist., Auct.
Antiq., xiii. 111–222).

and patriot, a disciple of Elbod, Bishop of Bangor. He was a man, he tells us, of little learning: they nearly all say that, and no doubt it was generally true. It was a part of the Christian humility, not now much exercised. As a writer, he would have us understand, he was equally contemptible. We are to pardon his barbarism and rusticity: a task not difficult, nor indeed to be too seriously undertaken when we find Tacitus in his *Agricola* appealing for the same mercy (*incondita ac rudi voce*). This is an older humility than the other, the ancient and justly suspected humility of authors, who commonly intend by such requests to draw attention to their obvious mastery over the language they employ. He wrote, this Nennius, as a lover of his nation, because no one else would; and from traditions, and such writings and monuments as had survived, put together, 'stutteringly', his version of the British story. From him we learn that the Britons came to this island in the Third Age of the world, and that it has its name from Brutus, a grandson of Aeneas, who settled here, and gave it the first regular inhabitants which it had had since the Flood. There is talk of Vortigern, and 'the boy without a father'—young Merlin, not yet fully named, the shifty Daniel of British prophecy. We hear, without relation to the Trojan dynasty, of one Arthur, a great soldier and Christian Paladin, twelve times chosen to lead the British against the Saxons, and twelve times victorious. In the last and greatest of his battles, at Badon Hill, he slays 960 of the heathen with his own hand. Legend was busy with him already. In some notes on The Wonders of Britain we read of a cairn with a stone on top bearing the footprint of a dog:

'This footmark on the stone was made by Cabal, the dog of Arthur the soldier, when it was hunting the boar Troynt.'[1]

The age of relics had begun, and relics mean romance,

[1] *Historia Brittonum*, ed. Mommsen (Mon. Germ. Hist., Auct. Antiq., xiii. 217).

but Nennius is not enterprising. You may read the story of that great hunt in the *Mabinogion*, but Nennius had heard of the dignity of history. Just as everything seems budding into the fable of Arthur the priest stops, and falls to mumbling some Saxon genealogies. It is undoubtedly a disappointment. We leave Nennius, who has nothing more to tell us. He had not done much, but he had done enough.

More than three centuries passed before another man arose who could talk of Trojan Britain, but he was the best, and indeed the grand authority on this subject: Geoffrey of Monmouth, also a priest, also a Welshman, and before he died, a Bishop. Geoffrey's *History of the Kings of Britain*,[1] composed in tolerable Latin of the time (*vili licet stilo*, he says, not meaning this at all), was known in the first draft by about 1136-8, and was the literary event of the age. Within twenty years it had been twice translated or adapted into French, and it raised such a hubbub among the other historians (and the twelfth century was full of them) that perhaps no other proof is necessary of its success. The origin of the book is simply stated in the Dedication.

'After much and frequent consideration with myself, upon my reading the History of the Kings of Britain, I wondered that in the account which Gildas and Bede had elegantly given of them, I found nothing said of those Kings who lived here before the Incarnation of Christ, nor yet of Arthur, and many others who succeeded after the Incarnation; though their actions not only deserved eternal fame, but were celebrated by many people in a pleasant manner and by heart, as if they had been written. While I was intent upon these and such like thoughts, Walter, Archdeacon of Oxford, a master of eloquence and highly skilled in foreign histories, offered me a very ancient Book in the British tongue, which in a continued regular story and handsome style, related the Actions of them all, from Brutus, the first of the Britons, down to Cadwallader, the son of Cadwallo.

[1] *Historia regum Britanniae*, ed. San-Marte, 1854; tr. Aaron Thompson, 1718, Giles, 1848, Evans, 1903.

At his request, therefore, though I had not made fine language
my study, namely, by collecting florid expressions from other
authors, yet contented with my own homely style, I undertook
the translation of that Book into Latin.'

This announcement, you will understand, made the
other historians stagger with envy. A real British
book, 'of regular and continued story', was what they
had all been looking for, and no one knew this better
than Geoffrey. The innocent candour of his Dedication is only to be interpreted by the glee of his Epilogue,
in which he speaks without disguises, rubbing his hands
in a manner by no means episcopal, and hardly becoming, in the circumstances of the case, even in an archdeacon. When he had finished his History, introduced
the first English King, and crammed what was left of
the Britons into Wales,

'as for the Kings [he says] that have succeeded among them in
Wales since that time, I leave the history of them to Caradoc
of Llancarvon, my contemporary; as I do also of the Saxons to
William of Malmesbury and Henry of Huntingdon. But I
advise them to be silent concerning the Kings of the Britons,
since they have not that Book writ in the British tongue, which
Walter Archdeacon of Oxford brought out of Brittany, and
which, being a true history, published in honour of the aforesaid
Princes, I have thus taken care to translate.'

It was quite true; he *had* taken care; and he had also,
as he knew quite well, produced a masterpiece.

Now, nobody enjoys having vinegar rubbed on his
wounds. Geoffrey's *History* was punishment enough
to the other historians without the sting of his epilogue,
especially as no one has ever seen that British Book, or,
I am afraid, ever will. We are on the borderland where
fable and history dance together to the first fiddle, and
Geoffrey is an orchestra in himself. To some extent,
no doubt, it was a joke of Geoffrey's, to exasperate his
fellow-professionals. Readers of *The Antiquary* will
understand the spirit. For the moment they did not

know what to say, and in Geoffrey's lifetime they
appear to have said little. It was announced, indeed,
later, in terms of some abuse, that Geoffrey was not
a wholly scientific historian; and this was difficult to
answer, because it could not be denied that he was
never uninteresting. Nor will the assertion of a recent
historian be easily shaken that 'the pages of Geoffrey
contain no new fact about the first five centuries which
is also true'.[1] And yet, that there were traditions of
British heroes, that Geoffrey, as a Welshman, knew
them, and that he anthologized and certified and (no
doubt) added to them at a time when they were
trembling on the brink of literature, these are themselves facts of some importance. It soon becomes clear
that we are not dealing with an historian, but with the
first and by far the most successful of our historical
novelists. The 'British Book', in all essentials, is our old
friend the faded MS., 'found among a heap of papers
as I was rummaging by chance in my uncle's bureau';
and his crony and compatriot, Archdeacon Walter—
historiarum peritissimus, a 'mine of old stories'—falls
into place as the possible Mr. Shortreed of Welsh
'Liddesdale raids'.[2] The Book itself is by no means a
total improbability, though it need not be supposed
that Geoffrey translated it. So far as he lied he was
a liar of temperament, with clerical precedent behind
him and the example of Ossian to come. A couple of
sheets in the Armorican or British tongue may by no
great stretch of the faculties, in a naturally warm and
enthusiastic mind, be imagined to be a Book. The
legends of his country, and sympathetic invention—
what Professor Murray has called 're-imagining your
sources'—were more than enough for the patriotic and
romantic task which was to occupy the remaining
leisure of his life.

[1] Haverfield, *Romanization of Roman Britain*, p. 88.
[2] See Bk. XI, ch. i, *ad init.*

The story of the Trojan settlement is told in full, and for the first time, in his opening chapters. Brutus, the great grandson of Aeneas, was expelled from Italy for involuntary parricide, and went to Greece, where he found a great number of his fellow-Trojans, descendants of the original captives, enslaved to the Greeks. He became their leader; was named General of the Remnant of the Trojans, as his descendants were one day to be Generals of the Remnant of the Britons; fought for their freedom, won it, and set out with them, as Aeneas his ancestor had done, to find a home in the West. We are witnesses once more of the universal desire of man to search out his origin, to find it in some great dispersion, and to look for the motive of it in the East. To medieval Europe, as to ancient Rome, Phrygia, by some epidemic taste, seemed to approve itself as the cradle of the western and elect nations. Brutus, like Aeneas, had an oracle delivered to him. He was told that he must seek an island beyond Gaul, in the Western Sea; an island where giants used to live, but now scarcely anybody at all (*habitata gigantibus olim Nunc deserta quidem*). To reach that happy shore, said the Voice, in surprisingly Virgilian language:

> To reach that happy Shore thy Sails employ:
> There Fate decrees to raise a second *Troy*,
> And found an Empire in thy Royal Line,
> Which Time shall ne'er destroy, nor Bounds confine.[1]

They had a good voyage, with few of the hardships of Aeneas and Ulysses; though this we should attribute, I imagine, rather to unfamiliarity with Homeric tradition than to any remarkable felicity of weather. Had Geoffrey been master of his commonplaces, that three-

[1] The Oracle is in the tradition. The title-deeds of all these Western foundations may be found in *Aeneid*, iii. 4–5:

> Diversa exsilia et *desertas* quaerere terras
> auguriis agimur divum.

days' storm which descends so infallibly on the epic voyager (*quarto terra die*) must have troubled Brutus also. As it was, his most dangerous adventure was with 'those Sea Monsters, called *Syrens*', whom Geoffrey, like a good medieval, conceives to have been a sort of feminist whale. They 'surrounded the ships, and had very near overturned them'. For the rest, he had the luck to fall in with four other bodies of Trojan exiles, moving in a kind of predatory partnership somewhere on the Biscay coast. The name of their commander was Corineus, 'a modest man, excellent in council, and of great size, courage, and audacity, who in an encounter even with a giant would immediately overthrow him as if he engaged with a child'. This Corineus, we are not surprised to hear, was by anticipation the first Cornishman, the inventor of the Hug. They celebrated their union in the usual way, and having raised the whole of Gaul about their ears, slipped off to sea and headed for the promised island, landing quietly at Totnes.

'The Island', says Geoffrey, 'was then called *Albion*, and was inhabited by none but a few Giants. Notwithstanding, the pleasant situation of places, the abundance of rivers and good fishing, and the engaging prospect of the woods, made Brutus and his company very desirous to fix their habitation there'. They drove the Giants into the caves of the mountains, and set so heartily to work that 'in a little time the country looked as if it had been long inhabited'. Brutus called the island, after his own name, *Britain*, and his companions *Britons*. But Corineus, in imitation of his leader, called that part of the island which fell to his share, *Corineia* (or Cornwall); and though he had his choice of provinces, 'yet he preferred that part . . . for it was a diversion to him to encounter with the Giants, which were in greater numbers there than in all the other provinces'.

Soon afterwards Brutus built his first city upon the

Thames and styled it *Troia Nova* or New Troy, a name
which it long held, till by corruption it came to be
called *Trinovantum* or Troynovant. This was the city
which Lud, the brother of Cassibelaun, afterwards
renamed Caer-lud, or Lud's City, whence London, and
Ludgate, where this king was buried. His family, we
are told, took it very ill of him that he should have
discarded the Trojan name, though in fact it was not
forgotten, but survived in the mottoes and pageants
of London till may-poles went out.

The line of British Kings thus founded by Brute
was long and distinguished. I could not hope to relate
the romantic adventures in love and war by which
their name was carried far beyond this island. The
northern peoples of Scandinavia, the tribes of Germany
and Gaul, and even Rome itself admired and feared
them. For they were great warriors, and of the best
blood in Europe. Names, as a historian of China
observed the other day, names are the music of history.
Epaminondas, Caligula, Tamburlaine, Hindenburg:
with such sounds one can build the groundwork of
a paragraph; and he sighs over those deserving but
unsonorous monosyllables, Chih Erh, Tz'u-hsi, Mo
Tzu. The mere names of our British royalties suggest
many things in tragedy and romance, and not merely
to English minds. There is Locrine, and his unhappy
daughter Sabrina, whom Drayton and Milton, Wordsworth and Swinburne have celebrated in verse; Leir
and his three daughters, Gonoril, Regan, and Cordeilla,
awaiting their passionate immortality; Gorboduc and
his fatal sons (whose highly unemotional names of
Ferrex and Porrex I should beg to exclude, however,
from this catalogue); Cloten, king of Cornwall, whose
son Dunwallo was the British Numa;

> Brennumque Arviragumque duces, priscumque Belinum.

Belinus gave his name to Billingsgate (which the

historian Green would unjustly assign to a Mr. Billing);
and Brennus (or Brennius) began life by going to
Scandinavia and marrying the king's daughter of
Norway, as the young men do in the ballads. There is
Morvid, and Elidure, and Peridure, who merely as
sounds will always fetch something in romance; though
if it be the part of a hero to die loftily, with memorable
words upon his lips, the romantic poet must handle
Morvid with care. His adventure was great in its con-
ception, but inglorious in its end. He went to kill the
sea serpent in the Irish Channel (it must then have been
almost in its first youth), and it 'swallowed him up',
says Geoffrey, 'like a little fish' (*tanquam pisciculum*).
I name without comment Gerontius and Cymbeline,
and pass to the final honours of the House. Almost the
last, and without comparison the most momentous of
all, come Uther Pendragon and his son King Arthur,
one of the Nine Worthies of the world, the hammer
of the Saxons, and the greatest conqueror, prince, and
knight in Christendom. As a young man, and between
times, he was as good at giant-killing as Corineus
himself, slaying in single combat the Spanish giant on
Mount St. Michael, and the giant Ritho, who went
about in furs made entirely of the beards of kings he
had killed. Responsibilities and honours grew upon
him. When he held his great festival and tournament
at the city of Legions upon the river Usk (Queen
Guinever or Guanhumara in her pavilion, and Kay
and Bedver already marshalling his court), all the
princes of Europe thought it their duty to attend, and
Geoffrey makes us feel that it was their privilege also.
He had carried his standard of the Golden Dragon to
victory over the known world, and had ventured to
oppose it, not without success, to the Golden Eagle of
Rome. 'You have made Britain mistress of thirty
kingdoms', he told his followers; and when he passed
with his wounds to Avallon, the Britons never recovered

from the blow, or took heart again except in the hope of his second coming. Some centuries of English indifference were needed to convince them even that he had died.[1]

There are other names in Geoffrey's book which have made their mark in less obvious ways since his time. It is a pleasure to find, in the list of the kings of Britain, two such names as Hudibras and Iago; and I cannot help thinking that Swift had heard of Gurgiunt Brabtruc and King Blegabred. Nor must I omit King Coel of Colchester, destined to be eternally old and merry, or King Bladud the patron of Bath, who was the first of our islanders to lose his life in the air. He flew over London and was killed, to the great astonishment of his subjects, who had always suspected that he was mad but had never known it till then.

There is no doubt that in all this fabling Geoffrey was something more than a lover of good stories. He was an enthusiastic patriot. The first words of his first chapter are more than a formula: 'Britain the best of islands.' He delights to relate how Belinus and Brennius (he is sure they were Britons) hanged the senators of Rome on their own walls; and how Julius Caesar was twice routed by Cassibelaun, and glad to put off to his ships again, 'rejoicing that he had the sea for his camp'. To be a British king, he reminds us, was the best stepping-stone, in later days, to becoming

[1] This belief was not invented by Geoffrey. It was before and after his time, and had its roots in the people. There was an outcry at Bodmin early in the twelfth century when some monks of Laon, visiting there, refused to admit that Arthur still lived (Ward, *Catalogue of Romances*, i. 217). And Archbishop Peckham, in 1284, complained to the Bishops of Bangor and St. Asaph (Geoffrey's old see), that the Welsh and English would never be at one while their parishioners so wholly addicted themselves to the Trojan visions, 'following the Brutan way' (*Bruti sequens vestigia*) (*Epistolae*, ed. Martin, Rolls Series, ii. 741–2).

Emperor of Rome. He makes the court of King Arthur the centre of all that was polite in Europe; even Rome seemed provincial to it.

'There was not a nobleman in the world who thought himself of any consideration unless his clothes and his arms were made in the same fashion as Arthur's knights.'[1]

So far did he go, indeed, in this direction that his critics in the next generation took to jesting with his name, Gaufridus Arturus, Geoffrey ap Arthur; and the stricter historians, while they continued to copy from his book, protested that his fables would be the death of history. They told stories against him. That 'brilliant and contentious half-breed', Gerald de Barri, writing his *Itinerary* towards the end of the century, relates of a Welshman tormented by unclean spirits that

'if the demons oppressed him too much, the Gospel of St. John was laid on his bosom, when like birds they immediately flew away and utterly vanished; but when that book was removed, and the History of the Britons by Geoffrey Arthur was placed, by way of experiment, in its stead, they settled in far greater numbers and for a much longer time than usual, not only upon his entire body, but even upon the book that was placed on it.'[2]

The historians must be forgiven their irritation, for Geoffrey had done what none of them had looked like doing. He had become enormously popular. That waggish style, so maddening to a rival, was not displeasing to the public.

'At this place an Eagle spoke, while the wall of the Town was building; and indeed I should not have failed to transmit the speech to posterity had I thought it as true as the rest of this History.'[3]

There is no contending with such a manner. The artist will not be denied; in this generous craft of lying

[1] Bk. IX, ch. 11.
[2] *Itin. Cambriae*, Bk. I, ch. 5, ed. Dimock, Rolls Series, p. 58.
[3] Bk. II, ch. 9.

the rest were cobblers to him. He had not only produced literature which everybody wished to read; he was
the cause of literature in others. The lost *Brut* of Gaimar,
the *Brut* of Wace, the *Brut* of Layamon (another Welsh
Marcher, and the greatest poet of his century), were
only the first of a long series of chronicles and romances,
not yet exhausted, which even when they invent or
improve still rest their fancies on the historical flowers
of Geoffrey. The chapters on Arthur so much derided
and enjoyed were the most fruitful of all; by the end
of the century the Arthurian Romance which he had
schooled and fathered stept out into the world full-
grown. When he died, in 1154, his book was so well
known that it was a mark of rusticity to be unacquainted
with it, and many had it by heart.[1] It had scarcely
been out when the chroniclers began abstracting.
Henry, Archdeacon of Huntingdon, happening in the
year 1139 to see a copy in Normandy in the Abbey of
Bec, was so profoundly impressed (*stupens inveni*) that
he made a summary of it on the spot, to go with the
later editions of his own History.[2] Geoffrey's boast was
fulfilled. He became the last word on British history,
and every British historian for four and a half centuries
had to repeat him, or be damned by the public as
jejune and incomplete.

It is noticeable that of all Geoffrey's critics not one
made any objection to his system. They railed at his
fables, but they had nothing to say against his Trojan
dynasty. They jeered at the marvels of Arthur (*Hic est
Arthurus de quo Britonum nugae hodieque delirant*), but
they had no complaint to make of the marvel of Brutus.
Even William of Newburgh, the most level-headed of
the twelfth-century historians and Geoffrey's bitterest
opponent, while he inveighs against our friend's

[1] Alfred of Beverley, *Annales*, ed. T. Hearne, 1716, p. 2.
[2] *Historia Anglorum*, ed. Arnold, Rolls Series, pp. xx–xxiv.

Arthurian generosities, only hints his disapproval of
the British Trojans.[1] So far as I know, the only Englishman before Camden who is said to have expressed
his doubts was the fifteenth-century historiographer,
Abbot John Whethamstede (Johannes Frumentarius),
by whom the world was not much moved. There were
foreign objectors, of course, but that was to be
expected. There was Polydore Vergil of Urbino, and
naturally no Italian liked to hear that the British were
as well descended as himself. For this among other
scepticisms, though his History of England (1534–55)
was the best that had appeared, and of most admirable
Latinity, he was treated as a man whom malice had
deprived of reason, and was vilified by British antiquaries for two centuries.[2] There was George Buchanan,
a Scot, and without denial an excellent scholar: but
what Scot ever lived, literate or illiterate, who could
put his hand on his heart and say that he had never
nourished a grudge against the English? Let him blush
to have thought *Tintagel* a man, and let him look to
the fable of his own King Fergus.[3]

There was also, in the next age, Peter Scriverius of
Haarlem, who pronounced it peremptorily 'a great,
heavy, long, thick, palpable, and most impudent lie,
and that so manifest as to need no refutation'; but

---

[1] *Chronicles of the Reigns of Stephen, Henry II, and Richard I,* ed.
Howlett, Rolls Series, i. 11–18.

[2] 'Homo ignotus et exterus', 'vir perfrictae frontis', 'infamis homun-
culus', 'os impudens', 'delirans Urbinas', are some nearly contemporary
flowers from the single nosegay of Humphrey Lhuyd. Polydore knew
what he was doing, having observed the effect of the British story on the
English people. 'They seem to be in heaven', he says, 'where with a
good will I leave them.' Nevertheless, he told the old story like the
others, 'albeit not altogether without indignation' (*P. Vergil's English
History,* Books I–VIII, ed. Ellis, Camden Soc., 1846, p. 33).

[3] 'Ubi ergo hominum illa portenta, Gogmagog, et Tentagol' (*Rerum
Scoticarum Historia* (1582), lib. ii, ed. 1715, I. 25). Buchanan knew how
to sting: 'Brutus parricida' (ibid., p. 24).

Dutchmen, it was well known, were better at drinking than at argument.[1]

You will readily imagine, then, the consternation of our faithful Troynovantines when Englishmen of acknowledged gravity joined the ranks of the sceptics. They appealed to patriotism. They represented the enormity of setting up a presumptuous criticism against the belief of ages. They dwelt on the danger of such modernism to history in general. Once more, as in Polydore Vergil's time, Brute was 'defended' and Arthur was 'asserted'. 'This man', cries Stow (still railing at Polydore, but with a rueful glance at Camden),

'this man with one dash of a pen cashireth threescore Princes together, with all their histories and historians, yea and some ancient Lawes also.'

The situation was desperate, and Stow prepared to discard. He would not now 'precisely defend' the descent of Brutus or the arrival 'by Oracle', but that about the time alleged 'there was one Brute or Brito king of this Realme', that he dare boldly say. Though Troynovant should founder the British pedigree remained.[2]

At the time it must have seemed a not unreasonable attitude. The new criticism was agnostic, and disparaging to the historical enjoyments of the nation: a nation for forty years and more, very conscious of its quality, delighting in its origins, and not least in those ancient heroisms and regalities of Britain. Chroniclers were in fashion in the sixteenth century, and in prose or in verse they had all been proud to tell the Trojan story. Holinshed is not less confident of 'Brute's coming hither' than Spenser is, or than the poets of

---

[1] *Tabularium antiquit. Batavicarum* (1612), Praef.

[2] *The Annales or Generall Chronicle of England* (1615), 'A Briefe Proofe of Brute', pp. 6, 7. Stow tries to dispose even of William of Newburgh as a foreigner like the rest, 'a French man borne as his name importeth' (William Petit).

A Mirror for Magistrates and *Albion's England*. Topography also had its Trojan patents of nobility. In the first Song of the *Poly-Olbion* (1613) Drayton makes the Dart claim precedence of all the Western streams because Brutus landed at her mouth,

'Which now the envious world doth slander for a dreame.'[1]

The first regular English tragedy had been of Gorboduc, and before the half-century was out Brutus and Locrine, Elidure and Lud, Lear and Cymbeline, Merlin and Vortigern, Uther and Arthur had all trod their hours upon the stage to the universal applause of patriotic playgoers. It has been calculated that the story of King Lear alone had been told by not less than fifty-two writers between the appearance of Geoffrey's History and of the old play which Shakespeare used. The stage was in those days the national lecture-room of history, and Heywood claims for the actors, with pardonable hyperbole, that as a result of their impersonations hardly a man was to be found by King James's time that could not 'discourse of any notable thing recorded even from William the Conqueror, nay, from the landing of Brute until this day'.[2]

It was no doubt some inbred feeling of these things that guided Camden and his fellows in their temperate statements of disbelief. Camden poses good-humouredly as a life-long friend of the Trojan story, borne down by the arguments of the judicious. For himself, he is a

[1] Drayton has no doubts. In the Tenth Song Brutus is 'the long traduced Brute', and every opposer of Geoffrey is 'our adversary'.

[2] T. Heywood, *An Apologie for Actors* (1612), Shak. Soc. Publ., 1841, p. 53. There was even boredom in the general proficiency. Hall complains:

'No man his threshold better knows than I,
Brute's first arrival and first victory.'
(*Virgidemiarum* (1598), Bk. VI, Sat. i.)

And King James had to submit to a 'Genealogy' worked out for him by a Cambro-Briton, 'with his lineal discent from Noah, in a direct line from Brutus, and from him to Cadwalader . . .' (1604).

'plain meaning man', and if any shall still declare for
the old Trojan faith, it is not he that will gainstand
them. Have every man his own opinion, or let 'the
Senate of Antiquarians' decide.[1] Speed is much less
affable, but Selden takes his tone from Camden and
refuses to be severe. 'That Arcadian deduction of our
British Monarchy' he would not, indeed, be thought
to support, and for the Trojan Brute he can argue 'but
as an Advocat for the Muse'; but he cheerfully anno-
tates the *Poly-Olbion*.[2] All three, and Stow and Drayton
with them, are swept and gathered up in that majestic
and reconciling pronouncement of which I spoke, in
the exordium of Milton's *History of Britain*. It is
long, but it is a luxury to quote it, and it sounds the
last post.

'Of *British Affairs*, from the first peopling of the Island to
the coming of *Julius Caesar*, nothing certain, either by Tradition, History, or ancient Fame, hath hitherto been left us.
That which we have of oldest seeming, hath by the greater part
of judicious Antiquaries been long rejected for a modern Fable.
Nevertheless there being others, besides the first suppos'd
Author, Men not unread, nor unlearned in Antiquity, who admit that for approved Story, which the former explode for
Fiction; and seeing that oft-times Relations heretofore ac-
counted fabulous have been after found to contain in them
many Footsteps and Reliques of something true, as what we
read in Poets of the Flood, and Giants little believ'd, till
undoubted Witnesses taught us, that all was not feign'd: I have
therefore determin'd to bestow the telling over even of these
reputed Tales; be it for nothing else but in favour of our
English Poets and Rhetoricians, who by their Art will know how
to use them judiciously.

. . . Of *Brutus* and his Line, with the whole Progeny of Kings,
to the entrance of *Julius Caesar*, we cannot so easily be dis-
charg'd; Descents of Ancestry, long continu'd, Laws and Ex-
ploits not plainly seeming to be borrow'd, or devis'd, which on

[1] *Britannia*, tr. Phil. Holland (1610), pp. 5–9.
[2] *Poly-Olbion* (1613), Introd., 'From the Author of the Illustrations'.

the common belief have wrought no small impression; defended
by many, deny'd utterly by few. For what though *Brutus*, and
the whole *Trojan* pretence were yielded up . . . yet those old
and inborn names of successive Kings, never any to have bin
real Persons, or done in their lives at least some part of what
so long hath bin remember'd, cannot be thought without too
strict an incredulity.

For these, and those causes above mention'd, that which
hath receiv'd Approbation from so many, I have chosen not
to omit. Certain or uncertain, be that upon the Credit of those
whom I must follow; so far as keeps aloof from impossible and
absurd, attested by ancient Writers from Books more ancient,
I refuse not, as the due and proper subject of Story.'[1]

Milton was both an historian and a schoolmaster. I
wish that modern historians and schoolmasters were
more of his mind. The British fables, in his opinion,
were too familiar, too attractive, and they had been
too much distinguished by literature, to be passed over
in silence even in a critical history.[2] Milton as a young
man had been in love with these old stories, and had
intended to do great things with them in poetry; but
on this matter the poets have always been sound. I
think of Wordsworth's *Artegal* as well as of Tennyson's
Arthur and Swinburne's *Locrine*, and I remember that
the other day we were reading *Lear's Wife*.[3] It is the
historians and the schoolmasters who have betrayed
us. I should like to see the Fables of the Britons
restored to their place in the first chapter of our histories. There need be no mistake; truth need not

---

[1] *Prose Works*, ed. Birch, 1738, ii. 2–3.

[2] See the original and characteristically conclusive paper by Sir
Charles Firth, 'Milton as an Historian' (*Proc. of the Brit. Academy*,
vol. iii, 1908).

[3] The full title of Wordsworth's poem is interesting: '*Artegal and
Elidure*. (See the Chronicle of Geoffrey of Monmouth, and Milton's
History of England.)' It was written in 1815, but long before that date
he had thought of attempting 'some British theme' (*Prelude*, i. 166–9).
Both to Wordsworth and to Swinburne the British stories were poeti-
cally sanctified as tales 'by Milton left unsung'.

suffer. Let the chapter be labelled—'Legends', 'Fictions', *Britonum nugae*, any defamation—and let Archaeology and Julius Caesar recover our senses in the next. We do this for the Grecian and the Roman fables, or at any rate we ought to; why not for our own?[1] They are as interesting as Livy's *primordia*; they were as devoutly believed; they were made from the same motives and by very much the same methods; and they produced a body of literature to which, if you except Virgil (and that, no doubt, is a formidable exception), Rome can show nothing comparable. If only Milton had written that epic he intended on the coming of Brute, or had broken, as he promised, the Saxon array beneath the warriors of Britain,[2] the balance would have been overwhelmingly Britannic. But there seemed to be a fate on our endeavours. Milton turned to other themes; neither Dryden nor Pope did more than 'plan'; and 'Estimate' Brown, who had Pope's design from Warburton, though he finished three Books of the intended Brutiad, collapsed with his hero at the Pillars of Hercules. 'So that, it seems, the Atlantic is the gulph of epic poetry.'[3]

---

[1] 'We are glad to notice from the specimen examination paper supplied to us that candidates are expected to know the principal tales of Greek mythology and legend. It was perhaps an accident that the paper included no similar question on the great legends of Roman history' (*Report of the Committee on the Position of the Classics*, 1921, p. 84). Was it an accident? Or are Roman historians following the bad example of the historians of Britain?

[2] 'Frangam Saxonicas Britonum sub Marte phalanges' (*Mansus*, 84).

[3] Rev. W. Gilpin to S. Rogers, 23 Jan. 1801 (*Early Life of S. Rogers*, by P. W. Clayden, 1887, pp. 416–17). Pope read Geoffrey of Monmouth in 1717, in the manuscript translation of his neighbour the Rev. Aaron Thompson, and translated the prayer of Brutus for him. 'The poor man is highly concerned to vindicate Geoffrey's veracity as an historian; and told me he was perfectly astonished we of the Roman communion could doubt of the legends of his giants, while we believe those of our saints. I am forced to make a fair composition with him, and, by crediting some of the wonders of Corinaeus and Gogmagog,

And here let me remark that the Trojans did not come to Italy in one way, and to Britain in another. After the great myth-maker Stesichorus, whose influence we calculate 'as astronomers infer the presence of an undiscernible star', it was Timaeus of Taormina who effectually planted them there and made a story of them, in the third century before Christ. He was the Geoffrey of those days, and the historians abused him in almost the same terms: 'that old gossipmonger.'[1] He is described by Mommsen as 'one of those historians who upon no matter are so fully informed as upon things unknowable', which recalls Haverfield on Geoffrey. But we owe the story of Dido to this good-for-nothing old inventor, and a number of other satisfactory things as well.

The contempt of history for fiction may be overdone. The hard-worked historian, in his excusable preoccupation with the truth, is inclined to be impatient of fables even when they are the fables of a race. It is a matter, partly, of expectation. Having trained himself to temperance, both to like and to locate cold water, he is professionally ruffled when the Geoffries hand him usquebaugh. But a myth like this of Troy, infectious, pervasive, European (for our vanity was shared), colouring men's sentiments, and in certain relations influencing what they did—powerful enough to make Homer the pro-Greek a suspected writer, and figuring solemnly in state documents—a belief of this kind cannot reasonably be dismissed like a bad answer in the class of history. However absurd it may have

have brought him so far already, that he speaks respectfully of St. Christopher's carrying Christ, and the resuscitation of St. Nicholas Tolentine's chickens. Thus we proceed apace in converting each other from all manner of infidelity' (Pope to Blount, 8 Sept. 1717: Elwin and Courthope, vi. 376). Thompson's translation was published in 1718.

[1] He had his William of Newburgh in Polybius, who went out of his way to warn readers against him, especially when he appealed to documents (Bk. XII).

been, it has claims on the historian because it was officially believed. The legend, as it happened, took richer forms in this country than in any other beyond Italy. Our pageantry of kings is a luxury of the island. But hardly a nation can be named in Europe which did not at some time aspire to this fraternity, and forge a Trojan passport. Francus of France kept company with his kinsman Brutus across the Channel. The good King Alfred was triumphantly derived from Beaw, the son of Ebraucus, the great-grandson of Locrine.[1] Even the peoples of Scandinavia, so remote from the Trojan circuit, and so handsomely provided with genealogies of their own, changed Odin to a King of Troy.

It has often been remarked with what singular good-fellowship the English and the Normans united their traditions and celebrated the same heroes. After the first rancour and disdain, the Normans adopted the worthies of England as if they had been ancestors, and were joined by the English in a common exaltation of King Arthur, who was a Celt, and had made his name by killing Saxons. This is a paradox which even the well-known impartiality of literature cannot wholly explain. Perhaps only Troy can reconcile it. On the Trojan assumption they had every right to pool their heroes, being distant cousins, and Arthur took his place in the joint Pantheon of the nation as the most distinguished Trojan of the north. It has been asserted, indeed, by Mr. Jusserand, that this fiction of a common ancestry was deliberately fostered by the Normans to make their conquest easy.

'Rarely was literature used for political purposes with more cleverness and with more important results. . . . Whoever the author may be, whether of French or English blood, the unity

---

[1] Beawivs 'qui fuit Ebrauci qui condidit civitatem Eboracum; et sic iste princeps inter mille nominatissimus Alfredus de natione venit Britonum, et sic de nobili sanguine Troianorum' (*Liber monasterii de Hyda*, ed. Edwards, Rolls Series, pp. 28–9).

of origin of the two races receives almost invariably the fullest acknowledgement; the inhabitants of the great island cease to look towards Germany, Denmark, and Scandinavia for their ancestors or for the sources of their inspiration; they look rather, like their new French companions, to Rome, Greece, and Troy.'[1]

Mr. Jusserand has a stimulating and heightened way of speaking, and naturally inclines, if there is tinder about, to make the Frenchman hold the match. The Norman nobles were probably less Machiavellian than he supposes. But the results which he describes can hardly be denied, and they deserve more attention than they have received.

In England the facts were not in doubt. Edward I and Henry IV quite seriously claimed the suzerainty of Scotland on the ground of the overlordship of Locrine, and the ground was not invalidated.[2] The household ordinances of Edward IV were based, with every symptom of decorum, on the precedents of King Cassibelaun and King Lud.[3] The Trojan story in all its branches became a family interest of the monarchy, and Lydgate's *Troy Book*, commissioned for Prince Hal, presented after his accession, and printed by order of King Henry VIII, turns out to have been an official as well as a poetical performance, a historiographer's service to the Crown. The Welsh House of Tudor had almost a duty in the matter, for its arms were supported by the British Dragon.

Whether we consider, however, the interest of the British stories themselves, over which we have been idling, or the occasion they have given for fine literature; or the great extent in space and continuance in

---

[1] *The English Novel in the time of Shakespeare*, 1890, pp. 40–3.

[2] Edw. I to Pope Boniface VIII (1301), in *Ypodigma Neustriae* (Memorials of Normandy), ed. Riley, Rolls Series, p. 220 f.; Henry IV to Robert III of Scotland, Aug. 1400 (Rymer, *Foedera*, viii. 155, 157).

[3] *Liber Niger Domus Regis Edw. IV* (Collection of Ordinances, 1790, p. 15 f.).

time of the Trojan belief to which they were allied, or the conviction with which that belief was held; from whatever angle we regard these things, we must conclude that they have been too hastily ejected from all footing in our histories, and, so far as they are stories, too unfeelingly withheld from the eyes of the young. It is about the young that I am most concerned, for the historians can look after themselves. And on that I have a moral for you, and an ancestor. There was an Englishman of the twelfth century called Lucas, mentioned by Saxo Grammaticus, the historian of the Danes. This Lucas attracted the attention of Saxo because of what seemed his odd (and possibly his English) combination of qualities: *literis quidem tenuiter instructus, sed historiarum scientia apprime eruditus*— 'not much education, but knew all the stories'. He not only knew them, but could tell them; and on a certain dark night in the Baltic, sitting with his Danish friends waiting for morning—all gloomy and silent, for they were raiding a pirate camp and things had not gone well—he so broke upon them with his stories and tales of old valour that they started up at daylight and slew the hateful Esthonians to the last man. 'It could hardly be believed, the strength that flowed into the minds of our fellows from the words of this foreigner.'[1]

I should like to see a little more of this Lucas in modern life: not quite so much education, and a better sense of the stories of the world.

[1] *Historia Danica*, Bk. XIV, ed. Holder, 1886, p. 583.

IV

CHARLES LAMB[1]

A VISITOR to London in August 1820 must have
remarked an unusual animation in the life of that
city. The season was over, but very few people seemed
to have gone. The theatres were still running, well
after their usual time, Mr. Kean announcing, for
19 August, his last performance in the character of
Othello before his 'positive departure' for America.
Wherever one went, in London or about, there were
soldiers quartered or on guard. It was said, with some
excitement, that a gunboat could be seen lying off
in the Thames; and there, sure enough, it was, facing
Cotton Garden, while a certain great lady passed
through the streets to the tribunal of the Lords
escorted by 'young men on horseback' and cheering
crowds of 'well-dressed persons' whom the *Courier*
called a 'mob'. We are in the month of the celebrated
Trial of Queen Caroline—the fourth act of a Royal
drama, never, perhaps, in the very best style, which
had swept all England into one gigantic Chorus, and
by something, we must suppose, Corinthian in its
proportions, had roused the least worldly of statists,
first gentleman of London, modest-hearted Ch— L—b,
to the chivalry of invective rhyme. He who had
declined six years before to triumph with his countrymen over Napoleon's fall, because the man was great
and in the dust, and persisted in liking men who
'frowned upon Trafalgar'—who in earlier days, in the
very chaos and thunder of the new-born world, had
found Burnet's 'Own Times' more seasonable than all
that the friends of the Revolution could write—this

---

[1] Centenary article on the *Essays of Elia* in *The Times Literary
Supplement*, August 1920; reprinted in Clarendon English Series, *Lamb*.

generous and homely freethinker was for once with
the majority. There was only one side for him, the side
of the weak, and he was a 'Queen's man' always.

It will be readily understood that no other topic, at
such a time, stood much chance. Even the reported
opening of the Regent's Canal, that 'singular example
of British industry and enterprise', and the prophecy,
punctually fulfilled at daybreak on the 23rd, of still
another Continental revolution, failed to obtain that
share of public notice which Portugal and the engineer-
ing interests had a right to expect. Only here and there
a few idle people, neither of the great Vulgar nor the
small, lazily glancing at the current pages of the *London
Magazine* and voting it otherwise a weak number,
found time to ask themselves, and in the end to ask
each other, the unusual question, 'Who is Elia?' It
was a short article, or rather essay, of some four pages,
describing in an assumed character—for it was not to
be supposed that the man had been a clerk—and yet
it seemed not all invented—the life of a great house
of business fallen into decay; with commemorations,
quick and affectionate, of its inhabitants, a queer
assemblage—odd fishes, a lay monastery—and yet
perhaps to another eye they might have been dull
enough—now chirruping, most of them, in the shades.
The style of the piece was of an older fashion and yet
new, with such felicities of phrase and pretty rhetorical
modulations as seemed to smile back upon their maker;
a style now brief and plain, now running into little
catches hanging loose, one would say, upon the score,
yet somehow masterfully concerted, and knocking, it
could not be denied, most strangely at the heart.

'Reader, in thy passage from the Bank—where thou hast
been receiving thy half-yearly dividends (supposing thou art
a lean annuitant like myself)—to the Flower Pot, to secure a
place for Dalston, or Shacklewell, or some other thy suburban
retreat northerly—dids't thou never observe a melancholy

looking, handsome, brick and stone edifice, to the left—where Threadneedlestreet abuts upon Bishopsgate? . . . This was once a house of trade. . . .'

Can it be wondered that the question was asked, or that at this distance of time, surveying events from our centennial *speculum* or watch-tower, we pronounce this, on the whole, the question of the month?

The answer was scarcely more readily to be guessed at from the man himself than from the essay, though he was in London at the time (his yearly holiday over), and living, in free commerce with his friends, where in those years he most loved to be, in the general noise and resort of all London—'the individual spot I like best in all this great city'—among the theatres and flower-sellers of Covent Garden. Any one in the habit of traversing this region, says Barry Cornwall, by merely extending his walk a few yards into Russell-street

'might have noted a small spare man, clothed in black, who went out every morning and returned every afternoon, as regularly as the hands of the clock moved towards certain hours. You could not mistake him. He was somewhat stiff in manner, and almost clerical in his dress; which indicated much wear. He had a long, melancholy face, with keen, penetrating eyes; and he walked with a short, resolute step, City-wards. He looked no one in the face for more than a moment, yet contrived to see everything as he went on. No one who ever studied the human features could pass by without recollecting his countenance; it was full of sensibility, and it came upon you like a new thought, which you could not help dwelling upon afterwards; it gave rise to meditation and did you good. This small half-clerical man was—Charles Lamb.'

So Elia, in his day-hours, looked and moved. He was in the first novelty of the character; a man of forty-five, with his golden years unexpectedly opening upon him; heavily tried in what are called the sorrows of the world, but with a gift for consolations; his chief friend and life-long companion an elder and ailing sister only

less lovable than himself; enduring the drudgery of the
desk because bread, as he would say, was dear and
publishers the devil ('those fellows hate *us*'); with no
great love for the society of what are called 'good
people', but choosing his companions, his *intimados*, for
some individuality of character which they showed—
'if they liked something, if they took snuff heartily, it
was sufficient': in short, a whole man, moving firmly in
his orbit, devoted to his sister, his folios, his friends,
and his puns, and living, upon principles rather practised than avowed, one of the bravest and happiest
lives in England. 'His enjoyments are so pure and
hearty', a young lawyer noted in his diary of this year,
'that it is an enjoyment to see him enjoy.'

Why he dressed as he did, in this Quakerish or
Methodist habit, we shall perhaps never know; but as
he adopted the custom early, it is conjectured that a
distaste for change, or what he called uprooting, and
a dislike of being mistaken for a poet or one of the professed *literati*, may have had something to do with it.
It has even been suggested that there was a certain
modesty and order in the matter, as of one who retains
his rank. He was of humble birth, the son of a gentleman's servant, but in a happy and sometimes lonely
childhood had learned the power of the emotions to
annihilate distance. 'The solitude of childhood' (he is
speaking of Blakesware in Hertfordshire)

'is not so much the mother of thought, as it is the feeder of
love, and silence, and admiration. So strange a passion for the
place possessed me . . . I was here as in a lonely temple. Snug
firesides—the low-built roof—parlours ten feet by ten—frugal
boards, and all the homeliness of home—these were the condition
of my birth—the wholesome soil which I was planted in. Yet,
without impeachment to their tenderest lessons, I am not sorry
to have had glances of something beyond; and to have taken, if
but a peep, in childhood, at the contrasting accidents of a great
fortune.

'To have the feeling of gentility, it is not necessary to have been born gentle.'

This passion for places, and more especially for the places where he had dreamed as a boy, continued with him through life; growing stronger, even, as Time lengthened his perspective, and what had been the Present entered, without quite passing, the hither and romantic limits of Decay. He was fortunate in all his surroundings. The chance which elected that he should be born in the Temple, and should spend his schooldays in Christ's Hospital, passing, as it were, from cloister to cloister, must rank with the imaginative solitudes of Blakesware among the ennobling provisions of his life. He grew up grave and gentle, and by the accident of 'a spacious closet of good old English reading' into which he was tumbled early, formed a taste and judgement which in their maturity (and that came early) acted, his friends would say, with the almost mechanical certainty of instinct. Like his sister, he loved pictures, plays, and books, and talk; collected in time the shabbiest library of first-rate books to be seen; learned to smoke and drink his glass; and at about the age of twenty-five, with one reckless gesture, took all London—its crowds, shops, theatres, and sins— to his heart. He needed only friends, and long before he was thirty had amassed as varied and interesting a collection as any man in England. The one great tragedy of his life, of which it is almost cruel to say how much it taught him, touches a subject on which Romantic poets, in their higher despairs, have loved to dwell. There was a curse on his family, of madness; not Mary only, but the whole family was tainted. Even of his robustious elder brother, John (or James Elia), Lamb wrote, after his mother's death, that he 'feared for his mind'. He had been himself perhaps the first to go, and in a letter to Coleridge written soon afterwards—the first we have—displays at twenty the same whimsically dressed but rooted courage with which he was to face the world. After other matters— bills, Southey's Epic, and a schoolfellow's courtship—

'My life has been somewhat diversified of late. The six weeks that finished last year and began this, your very humble servant spent very agreeably in a madhouse, at Hoxton. I am got somewhat rational now, and don't bite any one.'

The fit appears never to have returned; but something of wildness in Lamb's eye and in his wit still slumbered. There was a vein of recklessness in him not easily schooled, and a certain 'painful sweetness' in his smile —a smile 'seeming saved out of the fire'—which attested a memory and self-knowledge. Could he have forgotten, his sister's almost yearly illness must have stamped the tragedy on his mind. His joy among his friends was the joy of a freed spirit escaping from care, 'as a bird that hath been limed'.

Of Lamb's own writings other than *Elia* few are now read, though some are unequalled of their kind. As a young man he was known chiefly as a poet and the friend of poets, and retained the character long after he had resigned the rod of poetry for the pilgrim staff of prose. It was a character not ill founded. Though he early relinquished the triumphs of verse, he never abandoned its consolations. All his life, when the fit took him, he would rhyme for the good of his soul, and while aiming at sincerity sometimes hit perfection. Two or three of his poems, the products of happy casualty, are as firmly entangled as *Christabel* itself in the English memory. His plays and tales and early essays have been less fortunate. Some were never successful; taste has changed; and in this matter of essays Elia has cut out C. Lamb. De Quincey, who knew *John Woodvil* by heart, scarcely expected to have followers. But the tale of *Rosamund Gray* has drawn fewer admirers than it deserves since the days when Shelley exclaimed upon its loveliness; and the *Reflector*

essays on Shakespeare and Hogarth are professionally
rather than generally known. In their day these various
productions brought Lamb some reputation, but more
abuse; and it is probable that when he collected his
works in the year 1818 he regarded his literary life as
closed. He was then forty-three, and already sighing
for the retirement which was to come seven years
later—for 'fine Izaac Walton mornings', in which he
should stretch himself as careless as a beggar—'walking,
walking . . . dying walking'. It was Hazlitt, we are
told, who induced him to come forward and join the
brilliant group who were making the new *London
Magazine* an event in literature. He was teased into
starting, and seems to have enjoyed from the outset
the luxury of his mask. His first essay was followed by
a second, his second by a third; and from that time,
month after month, a series of the most exquisite
sketches flowed from his pen, in a prose which for
expressiveness can never be surpassed. He warmed and
glowed in the dramatic haze; found himself 'the hero
of the *London Magazine*'; and all its readers clamorous
for his name. In this strife a generous nature loves to
be overcome. 'How I like to be liked!' he cried. He
had had so much injustice done him in his own name,
he said, that he 'made it a rule of accepting as much
over-measure to Elia as gentlemen think proper to
bestow'. Strangely enough, when the essays were
collected in 1823, *Elia* hardly sold. There had been
some hint of certain freedoms touching matters of
faith, of an expressed and passionate uncertainty about
the leaving of this green earth and 'the sweet security
of streets' for an unknown Hereafter. Some levity also
had been found where gravity should prevail; and the
book was blackballed by the Quakers of Woodbridge.
For whatever reason, it was not again called for until
1835, when Lamb had been a year in his grave. The
Last Essays, collected in 1833, went off no better. Only

in America, preternaturally alive in these matters, the
piratical issues of Philadelphia sold well. Lamb was
gratified; and for that reason, but no other, we may
with less reluctance congratulate America on the
annexation of nearly all his books. His midnight
darlings, his folios—huge armfuls—now rest in the
noonday repositories of the other side.

It was the opinion of Swinburne that no good
criticism of Lamb can ever be written because nobody
can do justice to his work who does not love it too well
to be capable of giving judgement. 'No labour could
be at once so delightful or so useless, so attractive or
so vain, as the task of writing in praise of Lamb.' It
is true, and may be confessed the more readily because
the best interpreter of Elia must be always Lamb
himself. The providence which endowed him fortunately decreed that he should be not only the best
essayist and autobiographer, but also the best letter-
writer of his time, and that of the many friends who
wrote about him, from Hazlitt whom he admired to
De Quincey whom he bantered, all should write well.
Montaigne is not more self-confessed, nor Boswell's
Johnson more evidently portrayed. Yet much remains
for intimacy. It is the exquisite secret of Elia as of
Johnson that every reader must discover him for himself, and think himself alone in the discovery.

There is an opinion about, based partly, it would
seem, on his originality and partly on the unprofessional and almost private character of his work, that
the writings of Charles Lamb 'form no integral part
of the history of English literature'; that he is 'not in
the main current, hardly even in the side current of
the great stream', but a kind of 'tributary backwater'
like Sir Thomas Browne. The *Essays of Elia*, says Mr.
Lucas, are 'perhaps as easily dispensed with as any work
of fancy and imagination in the language'. I confess
that I find this difficult to understand. It does not

seem possible that the best critic of his age, living, however privately and unprofessionally, in the very whispering place of movements; from whose casual observations neither Coleridge nor Hazlitt, the official interpreters of the period, disdained to borrow texts; the chosen gossip and counsellor, when they most needed counsel, of the Romantics of the Lakes; and one of the first leaders in that rejuvenation of Shakespearian and Jacobean study for which his age is still remembered and which is working still, not merely in the text-books, but in the latest verses of the latest of our poets—it does not seem possible that such a figure could be dispensed with from our histories of literature, and dismissed, with whatever garlands, to an ornamental exile with Sir Thomas Browne. I believe, on the contrary, that if Lamb were so dismissed his existence could be inferred; that even if he were removed it would be necessary to invent him. Too much has been made of the idiosyncrasies of Lamb's work, and too little of what is normally excellent in it. There is much in Lamb, even in the language and style of the *Essays of Elia*, which bears the stamp of its time. Elia is not all fantastic. It was not of his Essays that he was thinking when he declared his intention to cut the age and write 'for Antiquity'. When he wishes to do so, he writes like a man of his time. There are many passages in Elia, and even whole pages, written in the very idiom of the day (so, of course, as 'with a difference'), which Hazlitt might conceivably have written in his best moments, writing without a glance at old Burton, simply as well as he could—Hazlitt, that Lamb *in circumbendibus*, who kept the highway of letters in his time and was the direct and acknowledged descendant of Goldsmith, Addison, and Steele. The common advice to young authors, that to write like Lamb is the road to ruin, proceeds from the same confusion. His quotidian good sense is forgotten in the

recollection of his more abstracted musings and his
gambols under the moon. But Lamb was a master of
many harmonies; and there are occasions when he is
content simply to affirm. Let us by all means be wary.
But

'I never in my life—and I knew Sarah Battle many of the
best years of it—saw her take out her snuff-box when it was her
turn to play'

or

'I am arrived at that point of life, at which a man may account
it a blessing, as it is a singularity, if he have either of his parents
surviving'

or

'I have been trying all my life to like Scotchmen, and am
obliged to desist from the experiment in despair'

or even, to take a higher tone, such a portrait as that
of Coventry on the Temple terrace,

'whose person was a quadrate, his step massy and elephantine, his
face square as the lion's, his gait peremptory and pathkeep-
ing, indivertible from his way as a moving column, the scare-
crow of his inferiors, the brow-beater of equals and superiors,
who made a solitude of children wherever he came . . .'

the young writer who sets his cap at these simpler
felicities will never be brought by them alone to the
infirmary of authors. The finest of all fine things in
Lamb, his reverie of Dream-Children,

Here little Alice spread her hands . . .

is also the simplest of speech. To love Elia it is not
necessary to make him queer.

V

SHELLEY AND THE OPPRESSORS OF MANKIND[1]

WHEN I was honoured with an invitation to give
the Warton Lecture of the year, it was suggested
to me by the Committee of the Academy that the most
appropriate subject for such a lecture, in the year 1922,
was the poet Shelley. I agreed, though not without
misgiving. It is one thing to thumb one's Bible, and
join in that chorus to the Unseen which goes up from
the pews; but to conduct the praise, or, what is harder,
to expound one's faith from the pulpit—a man may
be excused some hesitation to whom this proposal is
addressed. The works of Shelley, and especially the
more visionary portions of his work, have been raised
by his students to the status of Apocalypse. I hesitate
to try my faith in the evidence of things which even
by them are confessedly half seen and heard, and by me
are sometimes neither heard nor seen. I am blinded in
that world of dazzling light which is his element, and
which they say is theirs, and am whirled into an immo-
bility of mind by a form of motion which is never-
ceasing, and is neither up nor down. I am lost in the
interstellar spaces of this poet, and long, against my
will, for the sweet security of streets and English lanes.
Shelley, by the nature of his vision, demands augurers;
above his ordinary readers and disciples he needs a
priesthood; and Time, which denied him while he
lived both priesthood and congregation, has long provided him with both. I do not know what presumption
is expected of me. I belong to a profession hardened in
audacity, whose business it is to invade the deserted

[1] The Warton Lecture on English Poetry, 1922. Reprinted from the
Proceedings of the British Academy.

studios of dead writers, and to be officially familiar with the minds of great men. But in this airy and boundless temple of the spirit of which Shelley is the harmonious builder and the raptured inhabitant I take leave not only to throw away my gown but to decline the surplice. If for one hour I must presume, I would have you imagine me a poor deacon of the order, and my station in the antechapel of this Wisdom.

It is a hundred years and some months since Shelley died—not fighting much, we may suppose, against the waves which drowned him, but accepting his certainty of rest and his chance of revelation. All his life he had played with death, and often longed for it; and at twenty-nine, a grey-headed stripling, having lived, he would say, to be older than his father, he found it easily enough. He died in what he regarded as exile, his death scarcely noted except by the little circle of his friends, and was outlived by all the objects of his detestation: by the father who had, as he believed, persecuted and plotted against him, by the lawyer who had declared him unfit to bring up his children, by the churchmen and reviewers who had reviled him as an enemy of Society, and, I need hardly add, since they are still here, by all those institutions, public and domestic, which he had made it his business from boyhood to denounce and defy.

There is some point, then, in a Shelley centenary, beyond the flattery of an immortal. No man of his age had higher poetical ambitions than Shelley, or preserved them under more discouragement. It is hard to write without the confidence of finding readers. But that debt has been paid. I am more impressed by another column of the account which gives a less certain answer. Here is a man of the greatest genius and sincerity, whose whole life, in every act and expression of it, challenged the beliefs and usages of the society into which he was born. We do not now dispute about the poetical genius of Shelley; but so far as I can see, after a hundred years, his challenge to Society still holds, and controls this ceremony. We are involved, it appears, in something more athletic than an affair of almanacs and panegyrics, a reassurance to the world of letters that there are still garlands, that genius is still noted though deceased. Some answer should be found to this challenge, or at any rate, since an answer may be beyond our powers, the challenge should be stated.

I propose to celebrate the centenary of Shelley in this sense, neither in the language of flowers nor in the language of the altar, but, so far as I am master of it, in the language of men. My subject is not simply 'Shelley', as I have allowed it for convenience to be announced. Public lectures on 'Shelley' are independent of centenaries, and as appropriate last year as this. My subject is that which the date and the occasion have irresistibly imposed upon me: 'Shelley and the Oppressors of Mankind.'

I suppose that every centenary, when the object of it is a man who fought and suffered for the truth, as Shelley did, carries with it, if not a challenge, at any rate a question to the new age. The important thing at this moment is not what we sophisticated people think of Shelley, but what Shelley in his admirable simplicity thought of us. It was Jerome of Prague who first, I believe, of our modern martyrs hit on this test of the centenary, announcing to his enemies before his martyrdom, *post centum annos vos cito*, 'when a hundred years have passed I summon you for judgement'. I propose to issue this summons, and to call up some of the defendants in the famous and still pending suit of Shelley against the World. They make a formidable list. First, the institution of the Family, as represented by the rights of a parent over his child; next, the School and the tyranny of Schoolmasters, with the lower empire of the lesser Ajaxes of the form; the University, and the loathed autocracy of Dons; all Government or Power not delegated and republican—Kings, Emperors, Nobles, Judges, with old father Antic the Law; all Priests and Churches of whatever organized faith; the religion of Christ, with all its hierarchy (omitting only from condemnation, because one had been kind to him, the honourable class of country clergymen); the institution of Marriage, and the fanatical convention of Chastity; all Nationalists and Patriots forgetful of their citizenship of the world; all War and Soldiers (though Sailors, oddly enough, even fighting Sailors, are permitted: such was his love of this island, and of our Provost-Marshal the sea); all Hunters and Slaughterers of our fellow animals, and that perversion of Nature by which man, departing from the temperance of his beginning, has fallen to the grossness of flesh and wine; all Comedy (for what is Comedy but a mocking of our poor deformities?): with a long line of diminishing and lesser evils, flanked by that general pest, the Casual Acquaintance, whom he thanked heaven he had never been wretch enough to tolerate. The degrees of his denunciation vary, but one and all of the delinquents are evil: the enemies, avowed or not, of the freedom and perfection of man.

The strength and vitality of the human soul is tested by its contact with institutions. One after another they present themselves to the growing man, claiming to subdue him and to use him. It is fortunate that the earliest of these claims is put forward by so mild and wholesome a corporation as the Family, for after the family has taken its toll most women and some men are never heard of again. Shelley from the first resisted capture: as a child, by something wild and lonely in him, not easily tangible by parents; as a boy, by the otherworldliness of all his hobbies; as a young man, on the bitter ground of principle, at the point of the sword. It is natural to the young to hate tyranny and love truth. But where, in that tangle of loyalty and laziness which we call Custom, this tyranny lies, and what manner and degree of truth is to be expected in the laborious expedients by which the human race contrives its comfort and survival,—these are matters on which age and youth will never see the same. Shelley was a reformer at his first school, and from that time to the end never came, says Peacock, directly or indirectly, under any authority, public or private, which he regarded with respect. All successively presented themselves in the light of tyrannies or oppressions. It was no small part, we may imagine, of his early delight in Chemistry that the study was forbidden; or of his pleasure in Astronomy that this instruction also was outside the school routine, and introduced him to the notion of other worlds at a time when he was becoming aware of the imperfections of this. Night, with its vast plurality of stars, became, says a school-fellow, 'his jubilee'. He was odd, affectionate, and rebellious, fighting then, as in his later battles of opinion, with the girlishness of open hands; and at the age of twelve had dedicated himself, in tears and solitude, with the din of petty tyrants in his ears, to a war of justice, freedom, and gentleness among mankind. The minds of children are profound. We must not call this dedication absurd. A stone had been thrown, and we are witnesses of the first eddy of the pool.

The happiness which he missed as a schoolboy he might have been expected to recover at Oxford; and for a time, in the unaccustomed and tranquil freedom of the place, Shelley was happy. But he was the precocious child of reason and reform. There is a stage in the life of every young man of speculative habits when truth seems ascertainable by argument, and ascertainable about ultimate things. Not the least of the characteristic glories of Oxford are founded on this delusion, which we call generous because, as a rule, it is a delusion of youth. It was an article of existence to young Shelley. He had the good or bad fortune to be born into an age not unlike our own, an ambitious and disappointed generation, when all power and all experience were suspect; and to enter Oxford before the establishment of that ethical, political, and metaphysical tournament in which, under kindly tuition, the sword of undergraduate controversy, licensed and scarcely blunted, now fights all day long and often far into the night. With what gusto and what effects of health would Shelley have rushed into this battle! He found himself, on the contrary—ablaze with argument, burning to convince and to be convinced, aching for the duel—without an arena or an adversary. The game of ultimates was not played, it appears, by the undergraduates of University College, and he was driven to conduct it, like a lonely chess-player, by correspondence and in the press. He wrote long letters to men whom he had never seen, and who, never having seen him, addressed him for safety as 'the Reverend'; and coming at last to the point, having convinced himself that belief is not to be commanded, he printed and circulated among the persons officially, as he supposed, best qualified to help him (such as Bishops and Heads of Houses), a short pamphlet, which was on sale in Oxford for twenty minutes, giving the grounds on which he found it difficult and indeed impossible to believe in the existence of a God.

'As a love of truth is the only motive which actuates the Author of this little tract, he earnestly entreats that those of his readers who may discover any deficiency in his reasoning, or may be in possession of proofs which his mind could never obtain, would offer them, together with their objections, to the Public, as briefly, as methodically, as plainly as he has taken the liberty of doing.

'Thro' deficiency of proof,
'An Atheist.'

This air of the inquirer who asks for help seemed, no doubt, to his judges an aggravation of insolence; but when all deductions have been made for boyish bravado, the probability is that it was merely sincere. One of the charms of intercourse with Shelley, his friends affirm, was the openness with which he responded to opinions opposed to his own. He had asked a question, and it was always a grievance with him that he had not been answered; that he was met, not with argument, but with expulsion. He was an inquirer all his life, and the most startling, most lovable and alarming thing about him was his sincerity.

His expulsion from the University was the first of many sentences of exile—from his home, from the respect of Society, and at last, as he believed, from England. The chief battle was fought out with his father, and I shall dwell on it a moment because it seems to contain all the rest. Age, authority, experience, custom, compromise, and, let me add, kindness of heart confront, in the muddled person of Timothy Shelley, the logic of the stripling, the inhumanity of the enthusiast, the terrible rectitude of youth. Shelley at nineteen demands lucidity; everything must be *proved*; the only password is *Q.E.D.* The word 'God' is faulty: it is a 'vague' word. As for 'obedience', it was a word, he told his father, which should never have existed. One should not order, but convince.

'You can *command* obedience. The institutions of society have made you, though liable to be misled by passion and prejudice like others, the Head of a Family; and I confess it is almost natural for minds not of the highest order to value the errors whence they derive their importance.'

Youth, as his father remarked, is 'not the season for admissions'. It was a situation unfavourable to both parties. Shelley saw himself in high lights, 'surrounded, environed by dangers', 'an outcast', yet defiant, a solitary figure against a background of tempest, standing 'as it were, on a pharos', and smiling exultingly at the billows below.

'Am I not the wildest, the most delirious of enthusiasm's off-spring? . . . Down with Bigotry! Down with Intolerance!'

Timothy the father did his best, in his kindly incoherent way, for the old order, and he failed. Henceforth his lawyer must see to it. It is a pathetic spectacle, this clash of two sincerities in one house, the young brain of the new generation pitted against the groggy heart of the old: groggy, but as we say, in the right place. I have never seen a hearty word said for old Sir Timothy, though Hogg the parodist had an inkling:

'I have sometimes thought that if he had been taken the right way things might have gone better; but this his son Bysshe could never do.'

A martyr cannot afford to make concessions; he may be benevolent, but scarcely kind. As Timothy expressed it in his own idiom:

'This misguided young man courts persecution, and which to him would be a favor.'

Shelley did not live long enough to experience as a father the problems which he had set as a son; but the old Family, though it came sadly to grief over Shelley, having no equipment or set of standing orders for such an emergency, got out of it fairly well in the end. Sir Timothy had no idea of forgetting Shelley's orphans: they are those 'poor little innocents', and the boy goes to Shelley's old school, and eats his mutton-chop, on the way, in the front-room of Shelley's old enemy the family solicitor. On the whole (and if you will read the letters of this time not long ago recovered from the solicitor's office, I believe you will agree with me), the Family wins.

When a man rejects his family, or is rejected by it, he inclines, if he be an enthusiast, to found a family of his own, for enthusiasts need sympathy. I do not propose to disinter the mangled question of Harriet and Mary Shelley. I am only concerned to point out the need which Shelley always felt, and which he variously satisfied, for some woman who would try to understand him, and his belief that when she ceased to try, or to be able to do so, the contract between them was at an end. There is nothing very remarkable in such a belief, as held by either party. It is common enough to-day. What is remarkable is that Shelley acted on it, and could not conceive that he could possibly do otherwise. Much more than by his boldness as a theorist we are impressed by his courage as an executant. It is the rarer quality. His theories, on Marriage as on Government, he took from Godwin; but Godwin was the officer who dictates ruthlessness from a cellar. He had never, like Shelley, the bright subaltern courage of the top. He was startled, as others were startled, by the promptitude with which Shelley, believing a thing to be right, immediately did it. Marriage, Shelley agreed with Godwin, was an imposition of the priests, and Chastity a condition as selfish as it was dull. Constancy he believed to have in itself no virtue. To promise to love the same woman for ever seemed to him not less absurd than to promise to believe for ever the same creed. Literally, he appears to have been of opinion, a man could not honestly promise a woman more than this: 'I love you until further information.' It was, and is still, an arguable position; but it was an inhuman belief so long as Society and the woman believed otherwise. Mary Wollstonecraft Godwin, as became her mother's daughter, was as much of an executant as Shelley, and that partnership was quickly made. He left Harriet as a sculptor casts aside his failures. We reflect on the uncertain fate of visionaries' wives: Shelley meditating flight while Harriet chose bonnets.

It is a pity that the friends of Shelley have written so

inhumanly and so dishonestly about Harriet. It really is
not necessary to defame Harriet in order to clear anybody.
Beliefs, in Shelley, had the force of passions, and he acted
on his beliefs. The scandal and misery of Harriet's death
drove Peacock to wish that Shelley could have remained,
to his survivors and to posterity, a wandering voice; that
he had been left unseen in his congenial region

> Above the smoke and stir of this dim spot
> Which men call Earth;

that he had been heard only in the splendour of his
song. It was too much to expect. Shelley had entered
the lists of Society, and both in theory and in fact had
broken, with every circumstance of publicity, a remarkable number of its most cherished rules. An
unfilial son, a professed atheist, unhonoured by his
school, rejected by his University, an adulterer, and the
deserter, if not the murderer of his wife—the avowed
enemy of all constituted power, in State, Church, and
Family—advocate, it was reported, of a polygamous
and godless Arcadia—and what was more, of remarkable good looks and distinguished birth—heir to a
baronetcy—a poet—and not yet twenty-three: the
alarmed and delighted gossip who sits within us all
could never have permitted so rare a prize to escape the
mortuary of authors! There have been many coroners
and many verdicts, but no judgement is much worth
reading except his own. It is to be found in his works.

I pass from Shelley the troubler of homes to Shelley
the politician. He had expected at one time to enter
Parliament, but a closer acquaintance with Westminster Hall determined him against a profession for which
it is impossible to suppose that he was intended by
nature. His father was a Member, and eagerly encouraged the idea; but he showed his son too much.

'Good God! what men did we meet about the House—in the
lobbies and passages! and my father was so civil to them all!'

He became, instead, a free lance. The Irish were agitating, and he was in the Lakes. He crossed, and spoke and wrote among them as if every man should be doing the same, and with a confidence which touched the veteran Irish that Justice had only to be seen to be acclaimed by both parties. He wrote and spoke well. His *Address to the Irish People* should be read by the much more numerous readers of *Queen Mab* who imagine this to be his only earthly method of political pronouncement. They forget that Shelley, though a republican poet, was also an Englishman, and sensitive by right of instinct to the simple needs of a political situation. The miraculous visions and monkish denunciations of his political poetry are absent from his tracts, which will usually be found to advocate a policy of moderation: Liberty certainly, and sometime, perhaps, a New World, but now, at this moment, whatever instalment of Liberty can reasonably, without violence or trickery, be obtained.

His political poetry is notoriously less restricted, and so far as it is political, has probably embarrassed more readers than it has enlightened. Truth and self-deception, blindness and vision, ignorance the most childlike and foreknowledge almost absolute were never so chaotically mingled in the melody of words. The forces of nature are not tidy; we must take the sand with the gold. It has been asserted, indeed, that the political interest which appears so prominently in the poetry of Shelley is misleading: that so far as *Queen Mab*, the *Revolt of Islam*, and the *Prometheus* are political, they are written against instinct. It may be so:

> Some thought he was a lover and did woo:
> Some thought far worse of him, and judged him wrong;
> But verse was what he had been wedded to;
> And his own mind did like a tempest strong
> Come to him thus, and drove the weary Wight along.

The story of the *Revolt*, says Mr. Clutton-Brock, is

packed with political action, 'but Shelley digresses from it as often as he can and takes no pleasure in telling it. He writes about the great wicked world of tyrants and slaves, as a monk, telling the life of a saint, might write of all the pagan wickedness of the Roman Empire. The monk would represent the emperor as a demon on his throne. . . . He would have no notion that emperors were often overworked men who did evil by mistake or from cowardice or ill-temper. He would conceive of them as persecuting the saints because they hated the light.' This is indeed what Shelley does, and not once but always. The weakness is radical, and sufficient to have ruined poems less tumultuous with beauty and the cry of prayer. The gorged and drunken Kings, the baleful and malignant Priests who represent, in the fiction of *Queen Mab*, the political and ecclesiastical tradition of Europe, cannot be dismissed as the passing nightmares of adolescence. Shelley, though he disowned the poem, never wholly outlived it. Othman the Tyrant of Islam with his 'Iberian Priest', and Jupiter the Tyrant of the Universe still spread the black curtain for the drama of dawn; still in his latest visions palaces are labyrinths of crime, and temples and churches the larders and cookhouses of corruption. As with evil so with good. Colours of Queen Mab's Arcadia linger in the detail of maturer prophecies. Though the stage widens and is at last the Universe itself, the babe, in these recovered worlds, still plays with the basilisk, no berry poisons or storm blows, and man, living softly on roots and water, finds government and war, marriage, commerce, and religion miraculously displaced by the universal regimen of Love. The new world of the *Prometheus*, however, is far from the Arcadia of *Queen Mab*, and farther still from anything which men can hope for within a time worth measuring. The passion for reform is lost in the rapturous contemplation not merely of the world made better, but of a better world.

And yet, the prose interest did not cease. The recent publication of his last and most elaborate political essay, written in 1820, *A Philosophical View of Reform*, proves his continued occupation with the practical affairs of the world at a time when his poetry seemed to be more and more withdrawing from them. The situation considered was very like our own: a tiring war followed by poverty and unrest, a stirring of the nations, and in England a double aristocracy, of old land and new money, with labour earning higher wages which somehow bought less food. As is usual in these prose tracts he has much to say that is both moderate and wise. He concedes a good deal: to birth, for example, and even to commerce.

'Though at the bottom it is all trick, there is something frank and magnificent in the chivalrous disdain of infamy connected with a gentleman.

'There is something to which ... it is difficult for the imagination to refuse its respect in the faithful and direct dealings of the substantial merchant.'

His wrath is reserved for the profiteer. He would have all men equal at once—in rights, but not in property. 'Equality in possessions must be the last result of the utmost refinements of civilization.' He would have universal suffrage, but slowly; woman suffrage, but not yet. 'Let us be contented with a limited beginning.' He saw and deplored the 'mine of unexploded misery' lying at the foundation of the new industries and regretted the entry of a utilitarian philosophy into 'the enchanted forest of the demons of worldly power'. But on the whole his word is hope.

'We derive tranquillity and courage and grandeur of soul from contemplating an object which is, because we will it, and may be, because we hope and desire it, and must be if succeeding generations of the enlightened sincerely and earnestly seek it.'

The last hundred years have realized some of his desires, and some, also, of his forebodings. In the

twentieth century, with added troubles of our own, we
contemplate ruefully the undiminished heap.

It has been a perpetual disadvantage to the reputation of Shelley that his interpreters have so seldom been
willing to take him into the market-place and confront
a worldly audience with him on its own ground. The
young revolutionaries have found him out for themselves, and now sing his hymns; but at the first coarseness
of scepticism his more professed admirers have been accustomed to fly off in a gale of lyric into the void. It is
related of Shelley that from childhood he 'told tales',
and also that no one had a greater horror of falsehood.
The plain man is puzzled. 'He was altogether in-
capable', says Hogg, 'of rendering an account of any
transaction whatsoever, according to the strict and
precise truth.' He would narrate as real events which
had never happened, and see things which competent
witnesses declared were never there. He saw blood, for
example, on the white hands of Church dignitaries, and
demons issuing from the mouths of Judges, and the
Kings of the earth walking most pitiably naked among
crowds who praised their clothes.

But he was subject, we are told, to hallucinations.
Men came, and said things to him, when it could be
proved that no man had ever appeared.

The hallucinations of Shelley are a part of the man,
an extravagance of his art. His instrument was vision,
and his delusions are vision working at the wrong time
upon the wrong material. We all tend to over-use our
favourite instrument; the orator who makes speeches
and the actor who makes faces in private life are guilty
of the same error as Shelley. Shelley the poet is not
touched by any hallucination that may be attributed
to him; but Shelley the citizen, no doubt, becomes
more vulnerable. I will make a concession. I will confess that the bitterness of Shelley against what he

called 'the withering and perverting spirit of Comedy' has sometimes seemed to me to be more than the altruist's protest against the mockery of the weak. In his character of enthusiast Shelley recoiled, and not wholly without reason, from the corrosion of laughter.

The opponents of Comedy are drawn, as a rule, from two classes. They are either Officials, representatives of Bumbledom (Policemen, Vice-Chancellors, or Lord Mayors), or they are Enthusiasts for a cause. They have, in other words, either something to conceal (and these are the Officials), or something, some movement, to promote (and these are the Enthusiasts). And both are uncomfortably aware that it is precisely from these two classes that Comedy draws her plumpest victims. Shelley in society was one of the least self-conscious of men: but he was aware of the danger, and if he saw it approaching shrank from it like a monk from the ribaldry of women. 'There was not much comedy in Shelley's life,' says Peacock. I am sorry that there was so little; that he descended so seldom from his aerial promontory to the levels of common life; that he turned his back on that by no means uninforming person, the Casual Acquaintance; that he laughed so little, and was so seldom laughed at by his friends. The only friends who seem to have attempted it (for even Byron was quiet when Shelley spoke) were Peacock and Harriet; and it was, I am afraid, by no means the least of the qualifications of Harriet's successor that she was constitutionally unable to see anything to laugh at. Many of Shelley's most voluble admirers have shared, and still share, Mary Shelley's disability. But I have yet to be convinced that they relish more on that account what was true and lasting in this great and ill-befriended man: his clear sincerity, his admirable unworldliness, and his radiant gift of song.

The last four years of Shelley's life were spent in Italy. It may be some consolation to members of my audience, weary of the visionary and cosmopolitan programmes of the day, to be assured that Shelley, though he made and shared such visions, and has been claimed as one of the founders of modern cosmopolitanism, regretted bitterly his Italian exile and was a good Englishman to the end. He had never, indeed, at the best of times, been quite able to live up to that mood of universal tolerance which he had set himself, and for which Englishmen in practice are so little remarkable. Even on his brief tour of 1816 his mind kept turning, he says, to one spot of earth and the thought of home. 'So long as the name of country and the selfish conceptions it includes shall subsist'—the Universalist says grace for the Patriot—England, he is persuaded, is of all countries the freest and the most refined. He cannot imagine that travel could ever teach a man to despise the country of his birth:

'Our poets, and our philosophers, our mountains and our lakes, the rural lanes and fields which are so especially our own, are ties, which, until I become utterly senseless, can never be broken asunder.'

Even in his *Philosophical View*, written two years before his death, in a scheme of things which *ex hypothesi* excludes or at any rate frowns on war, he speaks of a lost millennium in which

'our ships manned by sailors well-paid and well-clothed might have kept watch round this glorious island against the less enlightened nations'.

We rub our eyes, but there is no doubt about the sentence. It is in the great tradition of Shakespeare and Milton and the author of the 'British Grenadiers'.

His longing for the old places grew upon him.

'I often revisit Marlow in thought. The curse of this life is, that whatever is once known, can never be unknown. You inhabit a spot, which before you inhabit it, is as indifferent to you as any other spot upon earth, and when, persuaded by some necessity, you think to leave it, you leave it not; it clings to you —and with memories of things, which, in your experience of them, gave no such promise, revenges your desertion. Time flows on, places are changed; friends who were with us are no longer with us; yet what has been seems yet to be, but barren and stripped of life. See, I have sent you a study for Nightmare Abbey.'

He kept his home-sickness for his friend Peacock. Mrs. Shelley, who was fond of Italy and disliked England, believed, and was permitted to believe, that he shared her taste. He never had a home, in the English sense, long enough to make it one, but he knew well enough what a home should be:

'The shrines of the Penates are good wood fires, or window frames intertwined with creeping plants; their hymns are the purring of kittens, the hissing of kettles; the long talks over the past and dead, the laugh of children; the warm wind of summer filling the quiet house, and the pelting storm of winter struggling in vain for entrance.'

It would not readily be imagined by one who knew him only from repute that the writer of these words was Shelley. He suffered in a hundred ways from his old enemy Custom, which he now saw to be a more formidable opponent than either Force or Fraud, because the affections make their nest there.

The reproach is sometimes levelled at Shelley that he deserted his country; that whereas Milton, his fellow-republican, returned to England because of the troubles, Shelley left England for the same reason. But it does not appear to touch him.

'The number of English who pass through this town [he writes from Milan in 1818] is very great. They ought to be in their own country in the present crisis. Their conduct is wholly inexcusable.'

This would be extraordinary, when we consider where Shelley was, if it did not mean that he regarded himself as invalided and out of the battle, that he was already withdrawing from that mixture of energy and error which we call life. Peacock fancied that if he had lived out his generation he might have passed his days like Volney, looking on the world from his windows, and perhaps, like that 'or some other' great apostle of liberty, desiring that nothing should be inscribed on his tomb but his name, the dates of his birth and death, and the single word *Désillusionné*. I cannot believe that this is true or likely. I had rather think of him as he pictures Minerva in the sculpture in the Florence Gallery:

'The face . . . is animated with a profound, sweet, and impassioned melancholy, with an earnest, and fervid, and disinterested pleading against some vast and inevitable wrong. . . . Wisdom is pleading earnestly with Power—and invested with the expression of that grief, because it must ever plead so vainly.'

VI

SCOTTISH LITERATURE[1]

THE literature of Scotland is the literature of a
small country, poor and for the most part sparingly
inhabited, proud, passionate, and tenacious. This
literature extends in time, if the utmost stretch of
record be taken, over more than six centuries, and
exhibits, in its chequered but continuous course, all
the exhilarating contrarieties of the race from which
it has proceeded. It begins, characteristically, with a
patriotic lament, and rhymed taunts at the English. It
is an emphatic literature, emphatic and even violent in
it sobriety as in its joys. Now Reason, now Instinct, is
exalted, now the head and now the heels. No literature
in the world is stiffer-backed or plays more cantrips,
has more decorum or more scurrility, better sermons or
better songs. It can be realistic to the last hair, and
fantastic as a dream. The discourses of John Knox and
the poems of Robert Burns, the Shorter Catechism
and the *Life and Death of Habbie Simson, Piper of
Kilbarchan*, the *Minstrelsy of the Scottish Border* and
Chambers' *Encyclopaedia*, the *Edinburgh Review*, wild
Sartor and *Kidnapped*, all in their degree, and without ultimate discordance, represent the Scottish mind.
No Scot is surprised that the same man should have
written *The Cottar's Saturday Night* and *Tam o' Shanter*.
He recognizes too faithfully in himself the essential
material of both poems.

The literature of Scotland has throughout a patriotic
cast, and it was indeed cradled in patriotism. It grew
up with the nation, and may almost be said to have
been born with it, out of the stress and exultation of the
old War of Independence. If sparks of that conflict still

[1] Revised and reprinted from *A Scotsman's Heritage*.

glow in the national memory the reason is not only that the national memory is long, but that Wallace and Bruce, the prime heroes of the struggle, each found, and not too late, his heroic poet. Scottish literature begins effectively with Archdeacon Barbour's *Bruce* some sixty years after Bannockburn, and to the *Bruce* and Blind Harry's *Wallace* (so staunch is the Scot, and such an antiquary in grain) must be attributed much of the colouring and subsequent tone of Scottish sentiment. The *Bruce* is the better poem, simple, truthful, noble, stirring, a proper start for the literature of a fighting people. England, which has so much, has nothing in its kind to compete with it. It was the *Wallace*, nevertheless, the wandering minstrel's story of the less fortunate hero, which caught the popular ear. It is a remarkable fact, or would seem remarkable out of Scotland, that this fifteenth-century poem passed through more editions (so its editors assert) than any other Scottish book before the times of Burns and Scott, and until the nineteenth century, in a modernized form, was to be found in every cottage in Scotland. The effect of this diffusion is on record, for in one such copy the poem was read by Robert Burns.

'The two first books I ever read', he says, 'in private, and which gave me more pleasure than any two books I ever read since, were the *Life of Hannibal* and the *History of Sir William Wallace*. Hannibal gave my young ideas such a turn that I used to strut in raptures up and down after the recruiting drum and bagpipe, and wish myself tall enough to be a soldier; while the story of Wallace poured a Scottish prejudice into my veins which will boil along there till the flood-gates of life shut in eternal rest.'

When he came to write 'Scots Wha Hae', he borrowed the last stanza, he confessed, 'from the common stall edition of *Wallace*—

> A false usurper sinks in every foe;
> And liberty returns with every blow;—

a couplet worthy of Homer'.

The *Bruce*, though less in evidence, never ceased to be read and to feed tradition, and like so many other ancientries came to glory again in Scott, for he kindled his Lays there. It survives to-day in anthologies both Scots and English for its noble and characteristic address to Freedom.

Next to this spirit of patriotism Scottish literature is distinguished, and pre-eminently in its poetry, by a joyous and incorrigible domesticity, and by a corresponding reluctance to cultivate or even attempt the more sustained and dignified artistic forms. The Scottish Muse, unmatchable in her way and on her day, is, upon the whole, a lady of short flights. Songs and ballads, the best in the world, racy satire, and humorous or romantic tale, are her restricted but native and congenial kingdom. Early in its history, in the golden age of the Makars, when Scottish literature for the first time, under the influence of Chaucer, entered the European stream, there seemed a promise of the greatest things. Henryson and Dunbar were among the most accomplished poets that western Europe could then show, and almost nothing need have been beyond them had they been the equals of their art. But it was not to be. At the first chance off go the singing robes, which so well become them, and they are poking their readers in the ribs. All this is very Scottish and to me agreeable, but the price of it, of course, is no Miltons and no Shelleys. Scottish literature, it has been said, unless roused to the universal by love or war, seldom strays far from the village pump and the familiar gable-ends. Its favourite sentiments are of the ingle-neuk and the neighbouring burnside, or the fun and freedom of tavern, market, and fair.

The tone was set from the beginning:

> To dans thir damysellis thame dicht,
>   Thir lassis licht of laitis,
> Thair gluvis wes of the raffel rycht,
>   Thair schone wes of the straitis;

> Thair kirtillis wes of lynkome licht,
>   Weill prest with mony plaitis.
> Thay wer so nys quhen men thame nicht,
>   Thay squeilit lyk ony gaitis
>   So lowd
> At Chrystis Kirk of the Grene that day.

What reader does not detect in these fifteenth-century verses the very lilt and bob, the happy vigour and native realism which three centuries later we find in Fergusson and in Burns?

So of that noble poem by the Dunfermline school-master, *The Testament of Cresseid*, the part that most certainly marks its author as a Scot is the intimate and homely introduction. He is about to write a 'Tragedie', he tells us, but must confide to us first that the weather is bad, hail showering and blasts whistling, and that he is past his first youth and feels the cold. So he does the right Scots thing:

> I mend the fyre, and beikit me about,
> Than tuik ane drink my spreitis to comfort,
> And armit me weill fra the cauld thairout:
> To cut the winter nicht, and mak it schort,
> I tuik ane Quair, and left all uther sport,
> Written be worthie Chaucer glorious,
> Of fair Cresseid and worthie Troylus.

The national literature is cheered throughout its course by such cosy interiors, and by the companies commonly gathered there, driving the night on 'wi' song and clatter'.

It is a foible of the Scottish people that it must always have its poet, its accredited and licensed bard, to tickle its sides and assure it that 'a man's a man for a' that'. It found him first in Davie Lyndsay, and then in Burns. The great Dunbar, styled by Sir Walter 'the darling of the Scottish Muses', and of all the Scottish poets the nearest to Burns in range and power, was, it appears, not democrat enough. Sir David Lyndsay, one of the last and most vigorous of the Makars, was a radical in the century of the Reformation, and addressed his unsparing satires on authority to the appreciative ear of the Scottish people.

> Quhowbeit that divers devote cunnyng clerkis
> In Latyne toung hes wryttin syndrie bukis,
> Our unlernit knawis lytill of thare werkis,
> More than they do the ravyng of the rukis.
> Quharefore to colyearis, cairtaris, and to cukis,
> To Jok and Thome, my rhyme shall be directit,
> With cunnyng men quhowbeit it wylbe lackit.

Jock and Tam became his grateful and appreciative readers, and were pungently rewarded.

It shows the toughness of Scottish taste as well as the obstinacy of the national memory that Lyndsay, with all his ancient coarseness, should have maintained for two centuries, even among the precise, his position as the popular poet of Scotland. For that post, it must be confessed, there was little competition. Scottish poetry, so rich and promising in the fifteenth and early sixteenth centuries, and still carrying in its wallet, to be rifled hereafter, the anonymous masterpieces of northern balladry, went under in the Reformation, and, except for Drummond and his friends, the Anglicizers, and here and there some stray performances on the native reed, only emerged in self-conscious revival in the eighteenth century. The literary glories which in the seventeenth century distinguished the sister kingdom have no remotest counterpart in a Scotland devoured by the congenial bitterness of religious strife.

From that angry and barren period it is a relief to turn to the rising hopes of the eighteenth century, for in many ways this was Scotland's greatest age. Gradually, both at home and in the new partnership with England, the Scot felt his strength renewed. The change was noticed across the Border. The community of authors in which Dryden had lived was an English community. By Johnson's time it was threatening to become Scottish, and there was perhaps not a county in North Britain which had not sent its man to the English mart of letters. Suddenly, within a generation, the sister countries, for Ireland was waking too, let loose their young men on the Metropolis of England, and threw themselves into the current of English literature and life. It is a cardinal event in the history of this island, and the country most alive to it was Scotland. In every department of literature and learning English, Scots, and Irish may be seen, for the first time in our annals, working side by side, for the glory of their persons and their parishes, no doubt, but also for a certain general glory which may be called the glory of Britain. In James Thomson's poem it is Britannia, not England, who rules the waves, and it is a Scot who says so.

The first sign of this change was in the age of Anne, when Scotland sent Arbuthnot and Ireland sent Swift to the English parliament of wits. It was a powerful deputation, and Addison, as the representative Englishman, had some ado to maintain his country in it. In the third and fourth decades of the century the second and more characteristic contingent appeared. From all parts of the island they came marching, each with his clean shirt, his poem, and his hopes. When Home came up to offer his *Douglas* he was escorted on his way by six ordained ministers of the Merse; but this was pomp. Thomson was more natural. He came alone, like the others, with his *Winter* in his pocket, and a great curiosity in his eyes for the country which was to treat him so indulgently. He was received when he reached London by a Scottish patron, a Scottish printer, and a Scottish friend, and was a good Scot to the last, never shirked his vowels, and employed a Scots barber whom he called 'Wull'. He was one of a group of poets who studied landscape with northern realism and gave a new turn of nature and simplicity

to English poetry. He is also one of the first of those
Scottish exiles, since familiar, who under the Anglo-
Scottish banner have done honour to Scotland and
served the common cause of literature: an ancestor, let
us call him, of Stevenson, Barrie, and of Lang.

It is interesting to distribute the literary achievements of the eighteenth century[1] among the nations
concerned; for they had their provinces and their
peculiar gifts. About the novel there could be no question. Scotland had Smollett, whom it has never
heartily owned, though he was the first Scot to reach
eminence in a form of literature in which his countrymen have since succeeded, and was the first also of the
long line of Scottish master-journalists in London.
Scotland had Smollett, and Ireland had Goldsmith,
but England held the ground; Scotland's turn was to
come with *Waverley*. In drama the balance is altered,
for the best comedies in that century were written by
Irishmen, and perhaps the only good tragedy by John
Home, the Scot. It was characteristic that the Irish
and not the Scots should take the comedies. The Irish,
unlike the Scots, have the feel of the boards; a taste for
histrionics distinguishes the nation; and that colloquial ease in English which the Scot even now finds
difficulty in acquiring, came then and still comes without apparent difficulty to the Irishman who writes.
The almost ludicrous anxiety of the Scots of the eighteenth century about their idioms and their vowels,
their furtive lists of Scotticisms, seem to have had little
or no counterpart among the Irish. Goldsmith's brogue
and his English were equally pure.

It was in this period, and under the pressure of these
limitations, that our Scottish writers determined that
policy which was to place them, before the end of the

---

[1] The description of Scottish letters in the eighteenth century is
borrowed from an article of mine, 'Dr. Johnson and The Provincials'
in *The Times Literary Supplement* of 19 Dec. 1913.

century, at the head of some of the principal departments of British literature. Cut off from the colloquial
arts of England, but conscious of great abilities and
great ambitions, they remembered that in the world of
learning it is not necessary to be sprightly, that it is
enough to have thought and to be clear. They therefore sat down to make themselves clear on every subject
which can engage a thinking man. The overwhelming
success of the experiment must have astonished them
then as it astonishes now. In almost every branch of
historical, scientific, and philosophical learning they
took the lead, and almost before England had recovered
from its surprise Hume, Robertson, and Adam Smith
had entered the world of Europe as standard British
authors. Even when they were attacked or rivalled it
was usually a Scot who was found to do it. The only
serious rival of Hume's *History* was Smollett's; the
only serious critic of his philosophy was Reid. The
intellectual confidence of the nation, never at any time
slight, rose with its success, and was the motive of much
of Johnson's raillery.

Meanwhile, throughout the century, at home in
Scotland, a more intimate and domestic revival was
proceeding. The old literature emerged, the bold free-
spoken compositions of the Makars in their more
roisterous and cheerful moods, the songs and tunes of
the people, and, a great thing this, the secret wealth
of Scottish balladry. These had never been wholly out
of mind in Scotland even in the dreariest times, but,
massed as they now were in one anthology after
another, they caught the quickened national ear. There
was no resisting their verve and the swing and gusto
of their metres, and a new race of Scottish poets was
presently strumming to them. Allan Ramsay deserves
his place at the head of this revival, for, though he was
not the first of its anthologists, he was the most dexterous and the most poetical and saw further than his

neighbours into the future. The rest of the tale is known: poor Fergusson next, then Robert Burns. It is interesting to note how quickly all this told on England. There were as many English as Scottish subscribers for some of these national anthologies, and, as the century went on, the songs and ballads of Scotland made their way to the very heart of English poetry. King James's arrival in England in 1603 with half his kingdom at his heels and a bag of golf-clubs was nothing to this invasion. The sudden and startling apparition of Ossian from the Caledonian north, in an age which was rapidly ceasing to be the Age of Reason, confirmed the growing expectancy for what might any day come out of Scotland. The publication in the *Annual Register* of selections from Burns while the Edinburgh edition was yet new bears witness to a maturing relationship of the two countries, not only in the general things of the mind, but in the more delicate matters of the ear and heart.

It was a stroke of capital good fortune for Scotland, and, one must say, for the world, that Burns and Scott, the two greatest writers and in some ways the greatest men produced north of the Border, should have been born just as and when they were: first, the poet of the people to bless with the warmth of genius the recovered poetical tradition of his country, and after him the Sheriff, to give Scotland, from his stores of memory and observation, the portrait of itself flashed as only he could flash it on the romantic background of its past. Between them, this poet of our common humanity and this master of our chequered story by love and understanding embraced the nation. Even as revivalists they divided the field, Burns doing and more than doing for the songs of Scotland what Scott from his youth up was to do for the ballads.

Burns and Scott, alone of Scottish writers, have achieved a universal fame, and the societies which produced them are now hardly to be found. For half a century, throughout the maturity of these men, Edinburgh had been a literary metropolis, rivalling London and respected in Europe. Some of the grandeur of those days still lingers about the streets of Edinburgh, but it must be confessed that its substance is gone with the prime cause of it. Modern Edinburgh, it has been said, seems not to mind who writes the books so long as she gets the printing of them. It might have been thought that the genius of Burns would have opened new paths in poetry for his countrymen; but the work of Burns is not the beginning of a period, but its climax and close. The Scottish Muse has many things to her credit in the century and more since Burns died, but singly they are slight and innovate little upon the past. That romantic unification of the Scottish Highlands and Lowlands which Scott achieved, making them known to each other, might also have been expected to release some new amalgam of native literary power. But the effects of that beneficent change have been more apparent in the life and business of the nation than in its literature. 'It was only in the age of Sir Walter Scott', says Mr. Trevelyan, 'that England discovered once and for all that she was linked with a partner not inferior to herself.' It might have been expected that that late but decisive discovery, and the triumph of a time when Abbotsford was the principal shrine of British literature, would stir the younger pens of Scotland to some inspired and feverish scribbling for the honour of literature and the north. A little of that there was, but it could not hold. Scotland has produced since that time, and continues to produce, its occasional writer of genius, its Stevenson and the rest, but not one has kept his roots there and stayed where he was planted. Like Carlyle, the greatest Scotsman of letters since Sir Walter, they all go south, and are numbered with their English brethren. There may be wisdom as well as destiny in this; but it leaves Scotland bare and the old altars smokeless.

Signs are not wanting that these things are understood in Scotland, and that a remedy is being sought. The search will be salutary even if the remedy should not be found. The leaders of the quest have much to hamper them, for Scottish literary tradition is as narrow as it is illustrious. Can it be widened, we must ask, without ceasing to be Scottish? A country which has produced no epic, no national drama, no national vernacular prose, and which in lyric, where it is strongest, has never cared to attempt those elaborations of art which distinguish the highest performances of other nations, is ill equipped, it must be confessed, for new literary adventures. The ingrained Scottish habit of cultivating the old patch will be hard to alter. The first step, perhaps, is to secure for Scotland what has been missing so long, a national literary centre.

VII

'REDGAUNTLET'[1]

IT is a hundred years since *Redgauntlet* was published, and few of Scott's novels have worn better. This is not because it is well constructed or in any technical sense unusually provisioned against the damps of time. On the contrary, it has defects of structure and of method which would have wrecked any story less various and less vigorously populated. Thirteen private letters, followed by two chapters of narrative—seven chapters from a journal, and eleven more by the author recounting at long intervals the adventures of now one and now another character—two chapters of epilogue, and a conclusion by Dr. Dryasdust—this is an edifice at which the novelist of to-day, were he asked to enter and take possession, would lift up his hands. To make matters worse, its architectural deficiences are all explained. At every turn of the rambling and delightful building we are faced with labels of direction and apology. We are told why the epistolary method was adopted, and subsequently abandoned: it was popular, great men had used it, but it had the fault of prolixity and redundance, and even so was found unequal to telling all that must be told. 'With this explanation we shall proceed to narrate some circumstances which Alan Fairford did not, and could not, write to his correspondent.' When Darsie's Journal is reached, we are instructed that 'the continuation of this history assumes, with the next division, a form somewhat different from exact narration and epistolary correspondence, though partaking of the character of both'. The reader

---

[1] Scott Centenary Article in *The Times Literary Supplement*, 4 Sept. 1924; revised and reprinted from *Scott Centenary Articles* (Oxford University Press, 1932).

is increasingly reminded of what he should not have forgotten; he is supposed to be 'aware', and it is expected that he 'may recollect'. It is even hoped that he has formed 'somewhat approaching to a distinct idea of the principal characters', but in case this 'good opinion of his sagacity has been exaggerated . . . the following particulars', it is opined, 'may not be superfluous'.

We regard all this now as fussy and old-fashioned, and from a modern novelist it would scarcely be endured. The novel has been severely disciplined since Sir Walter's day, and the writer of novels has been taught to efface himself, never to apologize and never to explain. Yet how friendly and comfortable Scott's method is, and how easily its sometimes tedious courtesies are forgiven! His readers are his guests, and as he talks he casts an eye over them from time to time like a host who tells a story in his own house. The charge of structural incompetence is one of the oldest and commonest that have been made against Scott, and within limits he would have been the last to deny it. When facts had to be faced he was of Saunders Fairford's opinion, 'Better a finger off as aye wagging'. He had tried to be tidy, and we have his word for it that he had failed:

'I have repeatedly laid down my future work to scale, divided it into volumes and chapters, and endeavoured to construct a story which should evolve itself gradually and strikingly. . . . But I think there is a demon who seats himself on the feather of my pen when I begin to write, and leads it astray from the purpose. Characters expand under my hand; incidents are multiplied; the story lingers, while the materials increase; my regular mansion turns into a Gothic anomaly, and the work is closed long before I have attained the point I proposed.'

This is honest and to the point, and the most important item in it is the demon. A vainer man would frankly have pleaded inspiration, but Scott would only say

that there were times in his composition when he was
not his own master. Shakespeare also knew this demon,
and what bounties we owe to him! What racy scenes!
What unexpected flights! What a gallery of humours!
And how many unfeathered and methodical pens are
waiting at this moment, and waiting in vain, for his
demoniac incumbency! There is a vitality of creation
that laughs at methods, and such figures as Saunders
Fairford and Peter Peebles, Nanty Ewart and old Tom
Turnpenny, Hugh Redgauntlet and Black Colin Campbell overstep the litigations of art. They have the
demon of immortality in their bones. Even on this point
of method Scott's modesty is exaggerated, like the
charges of his critics. For, let him wander as he may,
the grand progress of the drama, if it cease to move, is
never more than halted, and at every approach of the
master sweeps with gathering majesty to its rest. The
tale of *Redgauntlet* is digressive enough, but the main
story of that unhappy house, though its course is
devious, runs clean and strong, and finishes with a fine
head of waters in the ocean of Lost Causes. Even had
it been otherwise, Wandering Willie's Tale alone, like
an amulet about its neck, would have preserved the
novel from decay.

It would be pleasant to linger over the theme and the
motives of *Redgauntlet*, to stir once more 'the auld
leaven' of the Jacobite enthusiasm, to follow in fancy
the casks of moonlight, and for the hundredth time
stand with poor Steenie in what *seemed* the auld oak
parlour before what *seemed* the Laird. We should like,
if we had time, to loiter in the musty environs of
Peter Peebles's good pleasure, and hear him, however
'how-come-so' (he was turned in his old age a little
'Fifish—a wee bit by the East-Nook or sae'), rehearse
his old story and swear his old oaths, 'By the *Regiam*'
and 'By the practiques', while the macer called his
cause. Or what better employment than to trace the

fine outlines of autobiography in the story of Alan and his father, of Darsie and Greenmantle, and the frugal life in Brown's Square? It has always been known that there is much of Scott's father in that 'good old-fashioned man of method' and ex-golfer, Saunders Fairford, W.S., who 'considered every moment taken from the law as a step down hill', would have 'shuddered at his son's acquiring the renown of a hero', and 'laughed with scorn at the equally barren laurels of literature'. Practical Scots fathers and their romantic sons have had hard times of it with one another, and neighbourly opinion has generally sided with the father. Of Alan and Darsie Lockhart has told us all that one need know, but there would appear to be mystification in the assignment of their characters. There is much of Scott in both: in Alan his steadiness, good sense, and fidelity, and in Darsie his love of day-dreams and romance and Ariosto, of black-letter and the tombs in the Greyfriars' Churchyard, of gangrel bodies and auld wives' tales, and 'the blawing, bleezing stories which the Hieland gentlemen tell'. Of the lady in the case, Greenmantle or 'the maid of the mist', let us remark only the lifelong constancy of Scott to the memory of a girl he had loved and not won, and the decency and reticence with which he preserved it. The public history of our Romantics is rotten with the green-sickness of pining youth, but Scott, in such matters was a contemporary of Dr. Johnson.

More than one plea has been made of late for a study of Scott's prose even by admirers who bravely admit that he 'could write abominably'. It is believed that at its best his writing will repay any analysis and stand the hardest examination. Should this be attempted the evidence of workmanship in Scott's manuscripts and proof-sheets, which are appearing more frequently in the auction room, ought not to be overlooked. The proofs of *The Betrothed* and *The Talisman* offered for sale

two months ago from the Milnes Gaskell library, with
the relevant correspondence of Ballantyne and Scott,
if we may judge from the preliminary account of them
in *The Times*,[1] would furnish an essay on the trials of
magnanimity. James Ballantyne was a free and irre-
pressible critic, but he meant so well that Scott was
easy with him.

> We'll try again,
> We dinna ken,
> We'll aiblins happen better

is his modest and twice-quoted motto. 'I have been
tossed up a half-crown,' he says, on some point of
difference, 'and the luck is yours.' When, betrayed by
the rigmarole of the historical style, he so far forgot
himself as to call Berengaria, the wife of Richard Lion-
heart, 'a Royal maiden,' the joy of J. B. was unlimited.
Scott had always a great respect for 'the average man's'
judgement. But there were times when he would not
yield: 'I am not like Mat Lewis, who would have made
his heroine blue . . . if he could have pleased his public.'

A history of *Redgauntlet* on these lines would be
worth having. The revised proof-sheets passed, about
the year 1890, into the possession of the late Mr. David
MacRitchie of Edinburgh, and were lent to Andrew
Lang in 1891 when he was writing his introduction
to the 'Border' edition of *Redgauntlet*. Lang noted
some of the more interesting of the proof additions
and alterations, and a more exact and detailed account
of them was later furnished by Mr. MacRitchie himself.[2] The manuscript has a more intimate history. It
was presented by Scott to Robert Cadell in 1831, and
remained as an heirloom in the family until November
last, when it was offered for sale, and with exemplary
promptitude and public spirit was bought and presented
by Mr. H. P. Macmillan, the Lord Advocate, to the

---

[1] 2 June 1924.   [2] *Longman's Magazine*, March 1900.

Advocates' Library in Edinburgh. There, by the cour-
tesy of the Keeper, who understands his treasures, and
evites, as Peter would say, no interrogatories, a pleasant
hour may be spent turning over the closely written pages.
The manuscript, which is complete, consists of 214
quarto leaves, uncut and unsmudged. The sheets are
written after the manner learned by Scott in youth, and
twice referred to in the story. When Darsie, composing
his Journal in captivity, congratulates himself on the
smallness of his script, and puts it down to his residence
in Mr. Fairford's house, where he was trained to
transfer 'as many scroll sheets as possible to a huge
sheet of stamped paper', he is recalling the filial
minority of his creator. It is perhaps an effect of this
early training that Scott punctuates so little; what
readers demand in that way was left, apparently, to
the printer. The writing is on one side, without break
or margin; footnotes and occasional afterthoughts are
added on the verso of the previous page; new para-
graphs are marked but not spaced. The convenience,
to a rapid worker, of this parsimonious uniformity is
evident. No time was wasted on scribal etiquette, and
the author was enabled by merely counting the pages
to reckon almost to a word the amount of his morning's
task.

There are few corrections in that portion of the
manuscript which I have examined. Unless goaded by
criticism, what he had once written he commonly let
stand. But the first eight or nine Letters reveal some
interesting hesitations, among others the preliminary
uncertainty of the novelist about his names. Darsie's
first Letter is addressed not to Alan Fairford, but to
Alan Fairburn, and the catchword to Letter II re-
peats the name in this form. Here ended, possibly, the
first day's writing. The superscription of Letter II
deserts Fairburn for Fairford, and the desertion is final,
but introduces unexpectedly a new uncertainty. Shall

it be Alan or William Fairford? Scott had written
'William', but immediately repented: the name is
erased and 'Alan' written overhead. The hesitation,
however, lingered. The page which follows is that in
which Mr. Fairford, senior (with a 'Ha, sir! what
says your advocateship (*fieri*) to that?'), triumphantly
demonstrates to his son the true nature of *Doch an
dorroch* from the famous decision by the town-bailies of
Cupar-Angus in the case of Luckie Simpson's cow.
She had drunk up Luckie Jameson's browst of ale; but
there was no damage, it was held, and nothing to pay,
'because the crummie drank without sitting down'.
Melted by this success, and relaxing his customary
formality, 'But come, fill your glass, Will,' the relenting
father cried, and Alan, it seems, did so without expostu-
lation. This is the last we hear of William. There is a
little trouble elsewhere over that ominous personage,
Mr. Herries of Birrenswork. He is 'Herries of Dryfes-
dale' when he first appears in Letter V, and so remains
until the seventh Letter, when Birrenswork occurs for
the first time. His nominal vicissitudes do not end
there. With his Lairdship assured he nearly loses his
surname, and is announced in Letter IX as a 'Mr.
Maxwell of Birrenswork', though he reverts on the
same page. The Redgauntlet connexion with the Max-
wells and Pate-in-Peril was possibly running in Scott's
mind, or was it a recollection of that 'pint or two of
Maxwell's best, out of the fifth bin', ordered from Mr.
Fairford's cellar for Birrenswork's chack of dinner?
'Birrenswork', it may be remarked, looks in Scott's
handwriting uncommonly like 'Birvenswork', and so it
appears in the seventh Letter in the 1824 edition.

There are other trifles, pleasant in the detection, the
innocent finger-prints of authorship. The inn where
Alan said good-bye to Darsie is a blank in the first
Letter, and only comes into being as Noble House in
Letter II. Scott had looked up the posting stages. The

thesis for Alan's trials is 'upon——, and is a very pretty piece of Latinity'. It was not until the proofs came that Scott dived at the title *De periculo et commodo rei venditae.* No baying of dogs, in the first writing, greeted Darsie at the cottage in Brokenburnfoot as he alighted from the Laird's charger, and it is characteristic of Scott that he should presently have felt this sort of greeting to be necessary. The 'two large Newfoundland dogs' were added as an afterthought to the group which answered 'my companion's loud whistle', and a consequential place contrived for 'the two large water dogs' by the Spartan supper-table of the Laird. (Students of Scott's style hardly need to be told that the dogs are the same.) Already, by mere force of adoption, they have grown to be the handsomest of their kind: 'I never,' says Darsie, 'saw finer animals.' Once at least in these Letters Scott deleted on proof a sentence from one of his numerous digressions. It is in that passage where Darsie describes 'the policy or pleasure-grounds' of Mount Sharon. After much talk of the Leasowes, and of Horace Walpole, Scott states what was presumably his own mind on a delicate and much-vexed question:

'In spite of spite I will always remain of opinion that in the neighbourhood of a mansion house (itself an artificial object) such decorations as terraces, alleys, fountains, and so forth, where vegetable and architectural ornaments are blended together, add dignity and interest to the whole, connect the reigns of Art and Nature, and prepare for gliding from the regions where the former presides into the wide extended dominions of the latter.'

It was the old way of thinking, and will never be out of date while the ancient models remain, and gardening and building are felt, as Temple felt them, to be sincerely related, to be singly and jointly 'a sort of creation, that raise fabrics and figures out of nothing'.

As he threw in the dogs, to make a scene melodious, so Scott may be observed splashing colours on his sky.

That is an important moment in the progress of a tragic story when the novelist with his paint-brush first challenges the night. The tone of *Redgauntlet* is to be set. The light fades; a storm is blowing up; the young man is alone on the sands. 'I crossed', says Darsie, 'over the open downs which divided me from the margin of the Solway.' It is that third Letter of his, which checks the sauntering pace of the story and launches the drama on its first act.

'When I reached the banks of the great estuary, which are here very bare and exposed, the waters had receded from the large and level space of sand, through which a stream, now feeble and fordable, found its way to the ocean. The whole was illuminated by the beams of the low and setting sun, whose rays glimmered bright upon the wet surface of the sands, and the numberless pools of water by which it was covered. . . .'

This was very well, but to the novelist's thinking not well enough. Something more must be demanded of such a luminary on such a night. He took up his pen once more:

'[The whole was illuminated by the beams of the low and setting sun] *who showed his ruddy front, like a warrior prepared for defence, over a huge battlemented and turreted wall of crimson and black clouds, which appeared like an immense Gothick fortress, into which the lord of day was descending. His setting rays* [glimmered bright]. . . .'

It is a sunset of the old school, florid no doubt, but then so is the sun. It is good Abbotsford and good art, and would have gained had the printer kept the 'Gothick' of his copy.

What follows is in the mode of which Sir Walter was a master. The scene is to be 'animated' for a momentous meeting. Immediately the foreshore swarms with horsemen, of whom one in particular, sitting tall and erect on a black charger which he manages to admiration, inevitably distinguishes himself as leader. Night falls, the wind howls, the rank and file disperse, when

suddenly out of the gathering shadows the black charger
and its rider gallop up to the wanderer, with an unex-
pectedness which had in it, surely, 'something wild and
ominous'. The black horse is now sable; the wind
pipes louder; and over the treacherous shore the tide
advances with a hollow, menacing, and melancholy
sound. Darsie the dreamer is lifted to the saddle, not
a moment too soon, is galloped off the sands and, somewhat gruffly, is invited to spend the night in the
horseman's home. 'But why was it, Alan, that I could
not help giving an involuntary shudder at receiving an
invitation so seasonable in itself? . . . Alan, there is
something terrible about this man.'

It is a wonderful method as Sir Walter handles it.
How well we know it, and yet how well it works!
Should any jaundiced reader think it a little overdone,
he will find, if he is observant, that our author was not
insensitive to such a possibility, and can supply the anti-
dote.

'I have looked carefully at the facts of thy last long letter
[Alan writes in reply], and they are just such as might have
befallen any little truant of the High School, who had got down
to Leith Sands, gone beyond the *prawn-dub*, wet his hose and
shoon, and, finally, had been carried home, in compassion, by
some high-kilted fishwife, cursing all the while the trouble which
the brat occasioned her.

'I admire the figure which thou must have made, clinging for
dear life behind the old fellow's back. . . . Thy execrable supper
of broiled salmon . . . may be termed a real affliction; but as for
the storm of Thursday last (such, I observe, was the date), it
roared, whistled, howled, and bellowed, as fearfully in the
Candlemaker-row, as it could on Solwayshore.'

Scott was never afraid of chaff, and no master of heroics
was ever better or bolder at cooling their heels with
anti-climax. There is only one difficulty about Darsie's
ride through the night. How came this young man,
who was neither farmer nor surveyor, to decide without

hesitation, in a fitful 'blink of moonshine', that the cottages and crofts of Brokenburn 'occupied a haugh or holm of two acres'? But Darsie writes some odd things, and for an Englishman born, though schooled, it is true, in Edinburgh, is singularly informative about Scottish affairs. Why tell Alan, for example, who was born and bred in Scotland, that his course was crossed 'by a deep dell or dingle, such as they call in some parts of Scotland a den, and in others a cleuch, or narrow glen'? Or that 'the smaller sort' of salmon were called 'grilses', when Alan had never heard them called anything else? Or that there was placed on the table 'a silver lamp, or cruisie, as the Scottish term it'? This was useful in its day to English readers, and is useful now to many who have not that excuse, but as correspondence it wants likelihood.

The most interesting and best known of the secrets revealed by the manuscript and proof-sheets concerns a passage, perhaps the finest passage, in 'Wandering Willie's Tale'. In the manuscript one figure is missing from the infernal assembly of the malignant lords and captains. The fierce Middleton is there, and the dissolute Rothes; the crafty Lauderdale, and Dalyell 'with his bald head and a beard to his girdle'; Earlshall and wild Bonshaw, and Dumbarton Douglas, and Claverhouse, with his long dark, curled locks, 'as beautiful as when he lived'. But of 'the Bluidy Advocate Mac-Kenyie, who, for his worldly wit and wisdom, had been to the rest as a god', there is in the manuscript no trace. Scott was inspired to add him on the proofs, with a by-thought, no doubt, to the Honourable Faculty of which Sir George Mackenzie was so brilliant an ornament, and to the Advocates' Library which grew up under his eye.

That library, through the munificence of an Edinburgh citizen, Mr. (now Sir) Alexander Grant, and by the skilful management of a benefactor already named,

is soon to become a national possession. But its character, I hope, will not be changed. Sir George, if he still
walks, would be displeased, and there are others, if not
of the faculty, yet representative of the law, Saunders
Fairford, W.S., and Peter Peebles, *dominus litis*, who
might take it ill. For it is certain that the shade of
Saunders, in snuff-coloured brown and a sprig of holly,
still steps unseen to the Parliament Hall, and that the
spirit of P. P., looking rather better than worse for his
dissolution, still crosses that Parliament Close 'which
new-fangled affectation has termed a Square', and peers
about as of old for his meridian.

VIII

POETRY AND THE MODERNS[1]

NEARLY a year has elapsed since I had the honour to be elected to the Chair of Poetry in this University, and I regret the mischances which have delayed until now my grateful acknowledgement of that honour, and this first direct assumption of its responsibilities. I have been guilty of the misdemeanour of ill health, in itself a form of incompetence. The statutory duties of the Chair, it is true, are not at first sight formidable, and to a bustling and industrious man of a quantitative turn of mind might seem such as even an invalid could perform. The obligation of one lecture a term (for the Statute prescribes no more) recalls, indeed, in the gentlemanly modesty of its demands, that vanished Peace of the Augustans in which this Chair was founded, and that professorial reticence, so nearly amounting to silence, which was for long (though now no longer) an Oxford characteristic. Yet the matter is not so easy. 'Nearly half a century has passed', said Robert Bridges, reviewing in 1909 some of the published Oxford lectures of the Professor of Poetry of that date,

'since Matthew Arnold broke the Aristotelian tradition of the Chair of Poetry at Oxford, and by a course of memorable lectures set a new model to his successors; more congenial, no doubt, to them and to their audiences, but becoming more and more difficult and exacting as, with the growth of Oxford, a company of hearers has been assembled with wider tastes and attainments than could easily be matched elsewhere; indeed there is no conceivable combination of excellences which could be in excess of their demand. Arnold at one stroke magically transformed a pedantic and scholastic exercise into a living

[1] Inaugural Lecture as Professor of Poetry, delivered before the University of Oxford, 3 December 1934.

expression of modern culture; but in suiting himself he did not
consider those who might follow him.'

He did not, indeed, nor very much perhaps did Mr.
Bridges when he penned these unnerving sentences.
Mr. Bridges was an undergraduate here when Arnold
lectured, and was to live through almost the entire
cycle of his successors, among whom, had he chosen, he
might so royally have been inscribed. I cannot question, therefore, his *summatio*. To the eminence of my
predecessors, which I was never in danger of forgetting,
I must add, as a further obstacle to self-assurance, the
ivory fortress of an audience the most accomplished and
exacting in the world, which no excellence can surprise,
for which nothing is too good or possibly good enough.
Yet I seem to recall, and from no distant past, the
spectacle of just such another audience as this, so
manifestly of all the talents, quite forgetting itself and
the intolerable width of its accomplishments while it
listened with unaffected satisfaction and even delight
to the Professor of Poetry of the day—Professor de
Selincourt, Professor Garrod, Professor Ker—to name
no more—as he unfolded the noble traditions of our
English verse, or traced the divine gift and mastery of
Poetry to its sources in the profound and secret places
of man's nature. Whatever diffidence I may justly feel,
I am disposed to take comfort from such remembered
scenes.

Walter Raleigh once declared, speaking from the
unaccustomed platform of the Congregation House of
this University, that all lecturing on English literature,
in England and to English people, trembled necessarily
on the verge of absurdity: not, he explained, because it
is more absurd in itself than lecturing, say, on Greek or
Roman literature, but the absurdity is more easily
detected. An extreme form of this difficulty is evidently presented by the subject which I have chosen,
and chosen, to be candid, with more thought for my

own enlightenment than for yours. For it is a subject on which it is not merely possible that the lecturer may be wrong, and his audience right: it is possible that we may be all wrong together. So companionable a risk seemed worth taking. Easier country was widely available to me, safer routes and surer landmarks: the *veteres poetae*, for example, named by the Founder as the normal territory of this Chair. But these, I thought, might wait. The subject of Matthew Arnold's Inaugural Lecture seventy-seven years ago was explicitly, I find, 'The Modern Element in Literature'; and not the least valued portions of the brilliant and searching discourses of a more recent Professor of Poetry, Professor Garrod, were those in which he turned aside for a moment to survey the poetic activity of our time, to wave encouragement to the younger men, or shake, on occasion, an admonitory finger. In addressing myself, therefore, to the fluctuating scene of the modern literary world, to its shifting perspectives and quivering sensibilities, whatever risks I run, I follow not inclination only, but good example.

Yet of neither my title nor my subject can I say that it has escaped what is for me the choicest luxury of Oxford, I mean, the ever-welcome and purging candour of my friends. I have been pelted with questions, as: who then, in the first place, *are* the Moderns (the Ancients they had heard of); but the Moderns—can there indeed really be such people? What upstart clan is this? And by what violent abstraction are they so named, and that term, in itself a kind of slang, applied (if it is applied) to one group of living writers rather than another? If, as they more than suspect, I mean principally to denote that oblique, equivocal, egocentric, Anglo-American, and wholly unintelligible school of poetry built in the eclipse, fathered and hatched in the waste lands of these whimpering, inhibited, post-war years, then they take leave to tell me

that my adventure is at once too partial and too bold:
too partial, because it must neglect, or dismiss to the
circumference, many good and modest poets more
skilled in poetry than in publicity; too bold, because it
is doubtful if for any man turned fifty the undertaking
is even practicable. For how can it be supposed that
an ear habituated for half a century to the regular
prosodies of the past should respond to the uncharted
rhythms of these modern ditties of no tone? Or that
a mind trained and sedulously schooled to look for
meaning even in poetry should so far relax that now
inappropriate vigilance as to be content with meaning's
elliptic and slip-shod relative, significance, and with
only glimpses even of her? Muscle-bound from stren-
uous companionship with more manly and orthodox
masters, can one hope to achieve, even if the achievement were desirable, that state of passivity, of relaxed
and dream-like awareness, essentially required, it is
claimed, for the appreciation of verse of which the
method is not discourse but mere succession, and the
effect (when, boredom and bewilderment apart, there
is one) a kind of graduated meagre emotional inunda-
tion? Am I, further, an anthropologist? Have I shel-
tered with the alert intelligences of my time under the
Golden Bough? The latest findings, also, of the famous
clinics of the Continent, am I acquainted with them?
And in the political train, the wide-world express,
heading for the land of universal and contented Beta
minus, am I a one-way traveller, and do I sit with my
face to the engine or not? For if I do not, but like
such other 'poor ostriches of temporality',

> Gazing at yesterdays, I squat back-first,
> Blindfolded into brand-new futures burst,

then, they understand, Mr. Auden will laugh, and say
that there is Death inside me, and that will be very
terrible.

Now all these things, they were assured, are propae-
deutically necessary to the understanding (if the term is
relevant) and the proper enjoyment (if that is the word)
of the Movement or School with which, as they suppose,
I am resolved to deal.

What was I, what am I to answer to this bombard-
ment? After due reflection, I answer, first, that my
intentions have been fairly accurately divined. Second,
that I have a good deal of sympathy with the views
expressed, which are generally those of my generation,
the Conservative case. Third, that, nevertheless, a
poetical movement which generates so much friction
must have energy in it somewhere, even if that energy
is illicit. And fourth, that I am unwilling to believe,
whatever the novelties and obscurity of the productions in question, that communication, even poetical
communication, can be so completely cut off between
one generation and another as the friendly warnings
which I have recited would imply. Let me recall, in
this connexion, the case of Gray and of two poems of his
which now, I think, give little difficulty. 'In 1757',
says Dr. Johnson in his *Lives*,

'[Gray] published *The Progress of Poesy* and *The Bard*, two
compositions at which the readers of Poetry were at first content
to gaze in mute amazement. Some that tried them confessed
their inability to understand them, though Warburton said that
they were understood as well as the works of Milton and Shakespeare, which it is the fashion to admire. Garrick wrote a few
lines in their praise. Some hardy champions undertook to rescue
them from neglect, and in a short time many were content to
be shown beauties which they could not see.'

The history of poetry is full of such episodes, and satires
may still be read, the work of outraged contemporaries,
on the metrical, linguistic, and intellectual obscurities
of Tennyson. It is not the business of poetry to give its
readers what they expect, but by assault or by siege to
force an entry for the unexpected, the surprising, the

impossible. That there are scattered over these islands traditional poets of possibly greater natural powers and of higher accomplishment and performance than this new movement (as it is called) in poetry can yet easily show, or has had time to breed, I should not dream of denying; nor that a large number of the new poets write very ill indeed, in language only approximately English, and in styles which seem addressed neither to the brain nor to the marrow. I am stirred, however, by curiosity. The traditional poets I think I understand; I can meet them at any time, and meet them half-way. But the new poets are a kind of research.

Let me begin by saying that to explain the general disturbance in English Poetry to-day it is not enough to point at Mr. Eliot, and call in that jaded culprit, the War. Some change of the sort was impending and preparing before Mr. Eliot was thought of, and the War in fact delayed it. At the little group who first called themselves Georgians it is the fashion now to smile. They are thought homely. But there were good poets among them, good then and good now, and most of the things they worked for are a part to-day of the creed of our modern school of innovators. It was in 1912 that the first volume of *Georgian Poetry* appeared, and from that time until the War a campaign for the regeneration of English poetry, on certain well-agreed lines, was vigorously conducted in their *Review*. It was a campaign for plain speech (no flowers), for the recovery in verse of greater freedom of speech rhythms, for experiment both in metre and in the possibilities of free verse, and, above all and comprehensively, for the exploitation of dramatic verse, and the ultimate creation of a poetic drama which should hold the stage and make the theatre what it had ceased to be since Dryden. In this last ambition they were disappointed, and Mr. Eliot, I see, after long and learned hesitation, is now just venturing to tread the same path. But in all their

experiments, in dramatic verse especially, they did
work of which the memory and value survived the
War. For a few years their fraternity was even renewed.

Looking back to-day at certain *naïvetés* of that campaign, of which I was an earnest spectator, I experience
something of the tenderness which a man may feel on
revisiting the scenes of his youth. It was a time of high
hopes. 'Novelists', it was declared, 'point to a Third
Renaissance in this age; art-critics declare an unex-
ampled activity among painters; music seems likely to
become the expressive art of democracy. London is in
the rebuilding. What of the poets?' If one smiles at
this, let it be ruefully. They even spoke, and spoke
repeatedly and without shame, of 'setting their eyes
towards Beauty', which, of course, definitely and detri-
mentally dates them; for Beauty, like its adjective, has
been on the Index as a term of criticism for ten years
now since the Cambridge analysts labelled them *emo-
tive*. One thing these Georgians did, however, which
their successors might well learn from them: they
everywhere expressed the deepest respect for the great
poets of the past and the older methods of poetry,
while insisting that the modern poet should no longer
either imitate or repeat them.

D. H. Lawrence was an early contributor, and Ezra
Pound, Mr. Eliot's fellow countryman, adjutant, and
metrical confessor, even then a travelling specialist in
poetry movements, and on the way to become 'the
Barnum of the modern literary world'—yet a poet, too,
in parts—was in at once with what he has never found
any difficulty in supplying, a Manifesto and Credo. I
note that he had the assurance to call Lascelles Aber-
crombie's work mediocre, and that he was trounced for
his impertinence by Rupert Brooke.

The two Masters or Patrons of this movement were
Robert Bridges and Mr. Yeats: the first because of his
known profound acquaintance and incessant practical

concern with nearly all their problems, the second because, alone of modern poets, he had put good poetry on the stage and made it pay. The first Georgian volume was dedicated to Bridges, and that was right, for he was the most radical and far-seeing of them all. In every art, when a great master or succession of masters appears, it will be found (he urged) that they so exhaust the material at their disposal as to make it impossible for any succeeding artist to be original, unless he either find new material or invent some new way of handling the old. In Painting and Music this was almost demonstrable to the uninitiated; in Poetry the law might not be so strict, but it still held. Bridges believed, and stated then and later, that English syllabic verse had long been in this stage of artistic exhaustion, and that serious rhyme in English verse was worn out. Since the scourging poetic triumphs of the great romantics our poets had been working not only with debilitated material, but with blunted tools. What was wanted was a prosody not syllabic but of stresses, which would admit, to the infinite refreshment of poetic utterance, admit and somehow govern, the whole wealth of the common and natural rhythms of our speech. Such a prosody might abjure rhyme, or at any rate reduce its status. But as yet no such recognized prosody existed.

Now if the Georgians had a fault it was timidity, and if the Moderns have a virtue, it is courage. The Georgians shirked that business, Bridges returned to his experiments, and Mr. Eliot, of Harvard and Merton, taking a route of his own, went to school to the French Symbolists in Paris. The result was presently known. The 'blunted tool' of which Mr. Bridges spoke was thrown down with a clatter, and *The Love Song of J. Alfred Prufrock* started a movement. With the appearance in 1920 of *Gerontion*, and of *The Waste Land* in 1922, Mr. Eliot found himself established, and

proceeded to divide with Mr. Aldous Huxley the interest
and even allegiance of intelligent youth. How did he
do it? Let me quote the well-known first lines:

> Let us go then, you and I,
> When the evening is spread out against the sky
> Like a patient etherised upon a table;
> Let us go, through certain half-deserted streets
> The muttering retreats
> Of restless nights in one-night cheap hotels
> And sawdust restaurants with oyster-shells. . . .

Not exhilarating; but in a world which gives us, it is
said, so little cause for good spirits, why counterfeit?
The verse, in spite of its spacing, and its designedly
dejected rhythms, has a familiar ring: Mr. Eliot had,
after all, done nothing very drastic. His French studies
apart, he had only been researching a little, like some
of his followers since (though they never mention it),
among the half-lines of *Lycidas*, and in *Samson Agonistes*, where Bridges was finding the matrix of a new
measure. He retains rhyme, for the pattern's sake, but
uses it in the unobtrusive Miltonic manner. In his
later work the rhythms are much freer and less tagged,
and this suits him well enough, for his poems are
invariably short, and his favourite form is monologue.
Like all good Bostonians he knows or knew his Browning, and that Victorian master and almost inventor of
the dramatic monologue must be counted among Mr.
Eliot's teachers.

What am I to say of Mr. Eliot's poetic method?
This, certainly, that to a student of modern French
verse it offers nothing startling. Mr. Eliot, in his poetry
as in his criticism, is a cultured and exacting tradition-
alist: he innovates with circumspection and an eye for
precedent. His method is the dream method of Mallarmé, skilfully transfused into English, and rendered
as a rule in that tone of glacial irony and unruffled
yet hopeless detachment which was characteristic of

another favourite of Mr. Eliot, the poet Laforgue. Mallarmé's method has been described as 'variations on a theme withheld', and the phrase is exact for Eliot: a series of images is presented, of chance analogies and free associations, and by their flash, as they just twinkle and go out, a principal thought or idea is illuminated which with patience, submission, and some after-play of ingenuity may eventually be discovered.[1] One trouble about this method is that if the poet is wantonly private with his associations the reader may catch nothing. Another is that one may penetrate the various parts of the poem and, by missing some signals, miss the intention of the whole. To a psycho-analytic age the game should have become easy; only, the poet must really play it. This difficulty of divining the whole intention is to be met with also in the analyses of psychologists, and in many modern novels. What we are looking for there is character, and what we find, in fact, is a series of states. We may know each state, but what is their sum? Is there a sum? The totality of character evades us. So in poems of this type. The succession we may be equal to, but what binds and unites the parts? Mr. E. M. Forster once wrote a novel on the text, 'Only connect', and one wishes one always could. But advice which may be suitable for the conduct of life, for the life of 'telegrams and anger', is apt to break down before the waywardness and frailty of this material. There is, however, as Mr. Eliot himself has noted, another lucidity. There is a kind of pattern which we perceive in our own lives only at rare moments of inattention and detachment. The pattern here sought is of that kind, and must be similarly obtained.

In the transplanted mode which he has chosen Mr. Eliot is a finished artist. The style is compressed and decisive, and easily equal to the play of contrast with-

[1] See F. Y. Eccles, *A Century of French Poets*, 1909, pp. 282–3.

out which his slender edifice of irony must fall. Irony
by contrast, of beauty with squalor and grandeur with
meanness, is the key to his work; and it is the spring of
the contrast to be abrupt. Fine! you say, and the next
moment your hat is in the gutter. His device for this
(and it is a device he overworks) is the trick of literary
allusion, which though it limits his audience flatters
what audience is left, and does undoubtedly save time.
'Sweet Thames, run softly, till I end my song!' he sings
with Spenser; only to show us next moment the litter
of paper bags and cigarette-ends after a river party.
There comes a glow, a flushed hint from Shakespeare
of Cleopatra in her barge, and in the next line all the
language goes flat, and you are in a vacant lot among
the cats. It is a subtle and persistent distillation of the
robust antitheses of Mr. Masefield's *Cargoes*: Quin-
quiremes of Nineveh, and Dirty British Coasters; ivory
and peacocks, and cheap tin trays. Our shoddy civilization is shown up.

Over his London—for he is a town-poet, and London
is his dejected citadel—there hangs perpetual fog,
through which we are conducted with fastidious dandy-
ism past all the staleness of its muddled and crowded
life, from the sad smell of yesterday's spilt beer and the

> damp souls of housemaids
> Sprouting despondently at area gates,

to the more mannered desolation of rooms where

> women come and go
> Talking of Michelangelo.

Thus, in his somewhat 'defunctive music', Mr. Eliot
pursues his theme, which is (or was) Futility. I say
'was', because Mr. Eliot is now a Churchman.

'It is a complex fate', said Henry James, 'being an
American.' Eliot, like James, seems bowed by 'the
wear and tear of discrimination', a result, perhaps, of
taking too solemnly the concentration required to

become a good European. One is reminded of Mr. Strether, 'the poor sensitive gentleman' in *The Ambassadors*. This anxiety to get it right is most evident in his criticism. He spends half his time defining, and to that pitch has he carried it that when Mr. E. M. Forster wrote a letter to the *Nation* declaring that, of all his contemporaries, Lawrence, just dead, had been the greatest imaginative novelist, Eliot felt bound to reply that two others had as much right to be so described, and to complain that the statement was meaningless unless the words 'great' and 'imaginative' were defined. This, I think, is not very English, nor is it very good sense. It is another part of his Americanism to force the cosmopolitan note. When he announced himself the other day as to be rated henceforth a royalist in politics, a classicist in literature, and an Anglo-Catholic in religion, he was being neither American nor English, but a little absurdly French. Only in France do men label themselves in quite this way; Charles Maurras may do it, but not John Doe or Richard P. Roe. His poems swarm with sinister foreign figures ('Chicago, Semite, Viennese'), and an awful familiarity is suggested with the seamier side of European life. It is evident enough, however, that Mr. Eliot's life has been, in fact, innocent, and that the bagnios of Europe, like life's eagles and trumpets, are known to him only through literature.

Mr. Eliot's most influential single performance is, without doubt, *The Waste Land*. I think he has written better poems, but perhaps that is only because I find them easier. By that remarkable exercise in symbolism Mr. Eliot established himself as the accredited poet of a wide-spread modern mood, and as the master of what in Paris would be called a *chapelle littéraire*. When this and the rest of his slender output had been digested a body of verse began to appear and is still appearing, of every degree of competence and imbecility,

all consciously inspired or affected by his characteristic attitudes and technique. The authors, mostly
young, though they have other and even divergent
allegiances, look to Eliot as in some sense their head.

To become an Ancestor in one's lifetime is a trying
part, but less trying, I should suppose, to Mr. Eliot
than to most, being as he is a man fastidiously private
and with a natural turn of mystery, or at any rate for
son propre mystère. Dr. Johnson recommended long
ago to authors (though the message has not carried
well) the great advantage of keeping out of sight,
alleging the example of the Oriental monarchs, whose
custom it was to hide themselves and to be known to
their subjects only in their edicts. It is a policy in
which Mr. Eliot needed no instruction, and has had
much to do with the singular serenity of his command.
His prestige as a poet is impressively buttressed by his
authority as a critic (though the buttress has sprung of
late some startling fissures), and claims in both regions
have been made for him which, even if they betray the
instability of enthusiasm, are still of note. Mr. Bonamy
Dobrée, writing not in a coterie magazine, but in a
volume duly imprinted at the Clarendon Press, gave
it as his considered opinion, as long ago as 1929, that
the criticism of Eliot, 'with its depth, its wide grasp,
its beautiful distinctions, its enthusiasm, and its justice,
is the most important in English since Coleridge wrote
the *Biographia Literaria*', and lest this might be thought
impetuous, 'I am not forgetting', he adds, 'Landor
and Arnold.' 'As to his poetry,' the passage proceeds,

'just as no critic can afford to neglect it now, I am sure that no
critic of future ages will be able to give it anything but a pre-
ponderating place; and I would be prepared to lay odds that
the year 1922, which saw *The Waste Land*, will prove to be as
important a year in the history of the development of English
poetry as the year 1798, in which Wordsworth and Coleridge
produced their transforming volume, *Lyrical Ballads*'.

Here, at least, is courage, though whether critical or uncritical only time can tell. But if even half of this be true, what better appointed leader could our young men have found to guide them across the last quaking prolongation of the decried Victorian era? For in such scurvy terms they describe this age.

I have not the time to do justice either to the number or to the quality of the young poets now writing. Their name is legion, and, though many are interesting, of course only a few are good. Much that they print seems easier to write than to read, and bears, as the phrase is, 'no verse necessity'. Some of it is nonsense, and being of that automatic kind associated peculiarly with the name of Miss Stein, it had very little chance of being anything else. That the repetition practised by this method is a thing in Nature cannot be denied. 'The cuckoo said "cuckoo" in the age of the Romans and says it still, 10,000 times a day. It has never occurred to him, and never will, that his meaning has been expressed. Nature tolerates the perpetual rehearsal, and every day gives him 500 caterpillars that he may have strength to go on with it.'[1] All that is true: but the purpose of Art is to do better than Nature, when Nature is stupid. Fortunately there are a number of young writers of poetry at the present time who are exempt from these extravagances, and pursue their craft with some measure of discipline and discretion. Of these the small public which cares for such things has selected as representative, and with excellent judgement, three men, Mr. Auden, Mr. Spender, and Mr. Day Lewis. On what they have done I think Auden the ablest mind, able but angry, and Spender potentially the best poet; but all are good,

---

[1] Basil de Sélincourt, *The English Secret*. It was not until this lecture had been delivered and printed that I discovered the authorship of these sentences, which I had read and enjoyed where they first appeared, in an (anonymous) article in *The Times Literary Supplement*.

and seem to know better than most what they are doing, and why. I think they tend, like others of their generation, to over-dramatize themselves. 'The Great War', says Mr. Day Lewis, 'tore away our youth from its roots.' They represent themselves—rootless, without background or spiritual home—as a kind of orphans of the World Chaos. This 'chronique orphelinisme' (Laforgue had a pierrot who died of it) gets a little in the way; their youth, I am sure, saved more roots than they are aware of or are willing to allow. The public, however, which in a matter of sentiment always knows what to do, has had the kindly thought of healing their wounds and comforting their loneliness by sending them always on together, hand in hand, a troupe of three. Mr. Day Lewis says that he cannot tell why this should have happened, and I give him a reason besides their manifest and typical merit.

Their decisive selection of Gerard Hopkins and Wilfred Owen to be, with Eliot, their immediate masters in poetry, I can do little more than mention, but in that also they are representative. I think that in certain respects some of his younger discoverers have misunderstood Hopkins, who for all his swiftness of flight and boldness in experiment is a Victorian still. But what splendid, irregular, and exciting booty he has been to them! Owen, on the other hand, now accepted as of all our War poets the saddest and wisest, the most gravely musical, indignant, and profound, has been understood and rightly valued from the first. What our poets have learned or sought to learn from these two men, in poetic attitude and resource, in artistic economy and discrimination, I must not now inquire. At some later time, perhaps, I may hope to speak of this, unless it should be thought that Mr. Day Lewis, in his recent exposition, *A Hope for Poetry*, makes such inquiry for the moment unnecessary. He gives there a full account of most of the modern poetic schooling,

and speaks of the movement as a whole, so far as it is a
movement, with a modesty and candour to which we
are little accustomed in that context. The reported
poetical revival of the present time, the assertion of a
new and commanding power among our younger poets,
the sudden prominence of himself and his friends, he
treats with a becoming reserve. Why are we being
boomed, he asks, we three?

'There is no living poet in English who has proved himself to
be of the stature of Yeats; nor can I see any post-war poetry
which exhibits the triumph of personality that we find in the
poems of Hardy; there is little even that shows a technical
virtuosity equivalent to that of De la Mare. If we compare Mrs.
Monro's anthology of *Recent Poetry* with one of the Georgian
anthologies, we cannot assert that the general level of technique
is noticeably higher in the former. On the other hand, there
does seem to be an increase in what we may call vitality.'

What admirable moderation! The sacred cause of
poetry, and the poetical ambitions and experiments of
our time, lose nothing, I am sure, by such sobriety.

The mention of Mrs. Monro and the Georgian
anthologies brings the argument of this lecture full
circle. Mrs. Monro is the widow of Harold Monro the
poet, the most active member of the Georgian circle,
and this book of *Recent Poetry* was published jointly
the other day with the Poetry Bookshop which he
used to run. The two movements join hands, and there
is no abuse. Wilfred Owen in 1917 was proud to be
acknowledged by the earlier group; in the perspective
of history this thread of continuity will be more evident, and the proclaimed disruptions of these post-
war years will assume more normal proportions.

In that perspective (unless Mr. Dobrée is right) Mr.
Eliot, on his present achievement, will occupy, perhaps,
a place not unlike Mr. Lytton Strachey's in another
sphere: that of a man of unmistakable distinction and
purpose who just hit his time, and contributed some

needed austerity and precision to English criticism, and some opportune subtleties and sensibilities to English poetry. Where his latest work will lead him, and his latest doctrines, I cannot tell, but it is clear that his new Toryism and almost public acceptance of the responsibilities of middle-age have discouraged some of his most ardent admirers. His more insurgent scholars are playing tricks already with the Ancestor's curtain, and he has been warned by Miss Sitwell (whose whispers are so inconveniently loud) that if he does not take care he may find himself dethroned. Into these coterie unrests I must not pry. I prefer to welcome, as a sign of that increased vitality of which Mr. Day Lewis speaks, the emergence lately in some of the poems of our younger men of a theme untouched by Mr. Eliot, the theme of England, and the growing belief among them, however derived, whether from the gospel of Lawrence or the circulation of their own blood, that in spite of news to the contrary life is strangely worth having, and that there are worlds in store.

Before I end, there are two matters to which I should like to refer: one, the relation of poetry, as it is now being written, to the modern public, and the other, the intolerance and want of perspective in much of the criticism now proceeding from our various literary groups.

For the first, has there ever been a time when more young poets were at work, and the public, the general public, less expectant? Of situations of this kind the explanation has usually been the domination of the public mind, or that fraction of it which can be spared for poetry, by some great and popular poetic figure. We are to-day, however, wholly exempt from this embarrassment. No such figure is now extant. Meanwhile between our poets and the nation a mutual retraction is at work. The old compact audience is

gone, and the poet, in despair of ever interesting a
public to which no recognizable identity can be given,
which is in fact a hundred publics, tends more and
more to retire into a sort of specialism. This difficulty,
of course, is not new in kind. When the splendid close
of Shelley's *Adonais* was sent to France in 1915 as a
Times broadsheet, an officer wrote back: 'I don't object
to this sort of thing myself, but my men are against it.'
The difficulty is not new, but it has been multiplied.
All writers feel it, our novelists keenly, but the poet
most. The result can be seen in a steady contraction
of poetic utterance, a reduction in carrying power, and
a growing absorption, in spite of some propagandist
motives, in purely personal effusion and the special
problems of poetics at the expense of what would once
have been regarded as the most elementary duties of
communication. We are in danger of arriving at a kind
of code or shorthand poetry, built on allusion, and written by specialists for specialists. Indeed many would
say that much modern verse had already reached this
stage. The public, meanwhile, or that portion of it,
even now not inconsiderable, which naturally turns to
poetry—which rushed to buy Mr. Housman's *Last
Poems* and Mr. Bridges's *Testament of Beauty*—this
public, feeling itself unregarded by our more modern
poets, quite literally not spoken to, is retiring from
the experiment puzzled and sceptical. It is comforted
by remarking that, economically considered, the position might be worse; that the stock of good and accessible poetry in the world is still immense, even if one
generation should add little or nothing to it. We still
have our cellars, with all the old vintages from Chios
to Chilswell.

This contraction of interest among so many of our
poets coincides, and not by accident, with a growing
restriction of the actual sphere of poetry. The other
forms of literature are spreading, and there seems a

danger of poetry being crowded out. The formal losses of poetry since the days of the Greeks—dance, song, and at last even scansion—have often been noted and deplored. But its losses in territory have been hardly less considerable. More than a century ago Shelley noted the invasion with alarm, and the advance has been persistent. It was from considerations such as these that the idea at one time spread over Western Europe—Hegel, Carlyle, and many others shared it— that poetry might go out altogether, become superannuated, as surplus to the working establishment of a progressive and scientific era. Its chief rival and invader to-day is, of course, the novel, which has already well beaten it on their latest common ground, the exploitation of the sub-conscious. But the novel in its power of assimilation is the amoeba of modern literature, and like that protoplasmic organism, when it finds a prey, 'flows round it, incorporates it, and oozes on'.

I have sometimes thought that the Abbé Bremond's crusade for Pure Poetry was in part a half-conscious recognition of this diminished state, and an attempt to organize and secure it: to form, among the big kingdoms of literature, a guaranteed and ideal duchy for poetry.

Mr. Richards of Cambridge, the consulting Don of our modern movements (all such movements have had them), has stated it as his opinion that the communication difficulty which I have been describing will probably increase for the poets of the future. We cannot deny a poet, he says, his natural and necessary resources on the ground that a majority of his readers will not understand. This is not his fault, but the fault of the social structure. He thinks it probable that poets will become 'not less but more allusive, and that their work will depend more and more not only upon other poetry but upon all manner of special fields of familiarity'. In fact, Mr. Eliot's way is only the ABC of the complications to come.

It may be so, but I hope that Mr. Richards is on the whole mistaken, and that poetry will never so completely retire from the life of nations and of the common man.

I spoke of the narrowness and intolerance of much of the criticism of the literary groups now vocal. Movements, whether for peace or for poetry, are invariably disfigured, at some point, by the exaggerations and false emphasis of adherents, of the 'frantically frontal'. It is natural to an artist, hotly engaged with his own work, to praise whatever helps him and damn everything that doesn't. 'Raphael is no good'—'Dryden is no good'—only because he happens at the time to be doing something quite different, and the old master merely gets in his way. For the aberrations of the professed critic no such excuse can be found. Dr. Leavis of Cambridge—who plays, according to Miss Sitwell (she acknowledges that she has a grudge against him) much the same part in the literary life of Mr. Eliot as that of the faithful Watson in the life of Sherlock Holmes—this gentleman, I am credibly informed, has recently declared his inability to perceive any poetry worth speaking of (with the exception of Donne and a few odds and ends) between Shakespeare and Gerard Hopkins. Hysteria, plainly, if this be true. But he is not the only invalid. Mr. Herbert Read, a person of some eminence, asks us to believe that the great bulk of our poetry since Shakespeare has been on the wrong tack. It is hard to interpret such pronouncements, but it is helpful to note that according to the same authority the history of English sculpture is an even more humiliating tale of wasted labour and misdirected talent. 'We may say without exaggeration [I quote his words] that the art of sculpture has been dead in England for four centuries, and equally without exaggeration . . . that it is reborn in the work of Henry Moore.' Evidently this is how Mr. Read's mind works in all departments, and handing out death certificates to whole centuries is for him nothing unusual. I should not much mind such extravagance if it could be isolated, if the matter stopped there. But it is infectious, and not only foolish in itself but the cause of folly in others. I was assured by an undergraduate the other day that Eliot's *Waste Land* is the greatest English poem since King's *Exequy*. I think I knew what he meant, but it was plain that he did not share my knowledge. One of the coterie fashions of the day is to belittle Milton, who is by implication omitted, I may remark, from the brief first-class lists drawn up, or rather indicated, by Leavis and Read. It is the mode in such circles to speak of Milton as a minor poet, as the tiresome maestro of a backwater, and of his Epics as extinct curiosities of literature.

It would really seem as if the average human mind, having only a limited force of appreciation, finds it almost impossible to like anything very much without at the same time disliking almost everything else. 'The Amateur of Brahms', I quote our Slade Professor, 'seems to spend more energy in decrying the music of Stravinsky than in praising that of his chosen master; the Tchekov devotee makes a point of fidgeting when watching a play by Rostand; the enthusiast for Donatello remains proudly blind to Rodin and to Maillol'. You and I, it may be hoped, are still able to enjoy, as our mood or the occasion changes, quite different poets at different times: Chaucer need be no bar to Shakespeare or Milton, nor Milton to Pope, nor Wordsworth to either. They need never interfere with one another unless we commit the error, so prevalent to-day, of subjecting them all to the same aesthetic theory. The trouble is there, and Strachey was right. The spirit of intolerance, after being hunted out of ethics as it has been from metaphysics, finds an obvious refuge in aesthetics. If we cannot kill it there, let us at least send it padding on its travels again.

IX
ANDREW LANG[1]

WHEN I was told, some months ago, that by the generous provision of the late Sir Peter Scott Lang an Andrew Lang lectureship had been founded at St. Andrews, my genuine pleasure in that event was at once heightened and diluted by the simultaneous intelligence that I had been nominated to give the first lecture. I dare not impugn the wisdom of the University in having honoured me with an invitation which I found irresistible. But I was then, and am now more than ever aware that there are many, in Scotland and out of it, and notably in St. Andrews, better fitted by personal acquaintance to do what is required of me, to present a character of the brilliant, whimsical, most various and most loyal man of genius in whose name this lectureship has been established, and in whose honour we are met. I am addressing a company which at the name of Andrew Lang becomes at once and of necessity a domestic circle, and I ask myself if I have the family right of entry. My knowledge of Lang is chiefly a knowledge of his works, and even that knowledge, as you may well believe, is incomplete. I cannot pretend to speak for the circle of his intimates, a circle always small, nor even for his neighbours, or his generation. And yet, I comfort myself, it is possible that the very deficiencies of my equipment confer a certain advantage. Neighbourhood goes, memories fade, and from the most vivid of personalities the contemporary glow departs. In the end every writer (more especially if, like Lang, he values his privacy, and declines to be Boswellized) must balance his accounts with a pos-

[1] The Andrew Lang lecture delivered before the University of St. Andrews, 1 December 1927.

terity which can only read him. I have heard much of
Andrew Lang from his older friends both in Scotland
and in England. I have been one of his admirers for
a quarter of a century, and with an admiration that has
long since passed into affection. But I speak, and can
only speak, for a younger generation which knew him
chiefly from legend and from what he chose to print.
It is at any rate a partial approach to the condition of
Prince Posterity, who has the whip-hand of us all.
Seventeen years hence, with merciless punctuality, the
literary journals of this country will be announcing the
centenary of Lang's birth, and the usual questions will
be asked. What, in fact, was that genius of which he
was so prodigal? And how has it worn? The answers
to these questions, to be satisfactory, must be made by
that still younger generation of which I am glad to see
so many representatives in my audience. I have no
fear, myself, of the ultimate verdict. Much, no doubt,
will go, but Lang's roots strike deep, and he will gain
both in strength and in quality as Time lops his branches.

I spoke of a Lang Legend, for he not only pursued
mythology, but in his own person, as Thucydides says,
'won his way to the mythical'. The Legend was still
flourishing twenty years ago, and I am not quite sure
what has happened to it. One form of it turned on the
amazing volume and variety of his production, his
almost riotous fecundity, and of this as of other
miracles there was not wanting a rationalist explanation. Lang, said these jesting Levellers, was a Syndi-
cate, like Homer. It was a remarkable testimony to the
powers of one of the hardest-working writers of his
day, but even as a jest showed poor discernment. The
most striking thing about Andrew Lang, more striking
even than his variety and multiplicity, is the unity of
his work: how, on whatever subject he writes, whether
it be Homer or Scottish History, Anthropology or
Golf, the whole man crowds in.

Other forms of the Legend had at any rate an ideal truth, figuring him as a kind of gruff and grizzled fairy trading between earth and elfland. This image or symbolical picture flourished chiefly in England, which somehow ran out of fairies and ballad magic after the sixteenth century, and has since contracted the habit of looking for both of them to us. 'Mr. Lang puzzled the Sassenach a little', says Sir James Barrie. 'Perhaps this is the first duty of a Scot. He was so prodigal of his showers, and so wayward. There was a touch of the elf about him.' Of the native branches of the Legend the less apocryphal portions will go on, I hope, in his sacred places, along with the choicer study of his works: in his native Ettrick, where he gathered those boyish treasures of possible and impossible loyalties which were to colour and even direct his life; in St. Andrews, where he first spread his wings, which was his first Alma Mater, his second home, and is now his resting-place.

He was an *alumnus* of three Universities, and it is well enough known which of the three he liked best. Though he enjoyed Oxford and made his mark there, and celebrated then and later the charms of her somewhat disdainful beauty, she had come too late. His heart was lost already to St. Andrews. At the Edinburgh Academy he had, like St. Augustine, 'loathed' Greek, but, more fortunate than the Saint, had been converted by Homer. Homer was to me, he says, 'the real beginning of study'. He carried further at St. Andrews his exploration of the classics, under the wise and kindly guidance of his uncle, Professor Sellar, and, guided only by himself and the Providence that waits on genius, read magic in your University Library and plunged into folk-lore. He played cricket also (need I say it?), and golf, and football, and by the light of candle-ends ('stolen', it appears) he practised, in St. Leonard's Hall, the arts of journalism. Add to this characteristic assembly of interests the devotions of a Borderer—the infant care of a Cameronian nurse, but a Jacobite as soon almost as he could walk—steeped from childhood in balladry and folk-tale and the lore of ghosts and witches, an angler, and sworn knight of the train of Sir Walter Scott: make up this sum, and between Selkirk and St. Andrews you have already, at nineteen, in his first state, as the collectors say, and with his edges still uncut, the Andrew Lang we know.

Of Glasgow University, where he spent a winter session, he has left no very attractive picture. It is excluded from his well-known poem of *Almae Matres*; to that happy plurality only Oxford and St. Andrews are admitted. Indeed I am at a loss for the moment to recall in his works more than a single voluntary mention of Glasgow, and even of that the import is dubious. It occurs in a piece in which he urges with great earnestness, and in very good Scots, that we should

tak' a seat and wait
For ye canna be ower late
When ye're waitin' on the Glesca' train.

Candour, as well as loyalty to my own first Alma Mater, obliges me to explain that Lang had gone reluctantly to Glasgow on a purely business errand, to qualify by residence for the Snell Exhibition. It is not surprising, then, that he found fault. 'The students of Glasgow University', he notes in his *Life* of Lockhart—it was the winter of 1863—'still wore the red gowns', but in what to an East Neuk eye seemed a casual and degenerate manner. Even the gowns themselves appeared 'very scrimped, in contrast with the flowing academic dress of St. Andrews'. He recalls 'the black old quadrangle, guarded by an effigy of some heraldic animal, probably the Scottish lion, in whose open mouth it was thought unbecoming to insert a bun.

Blackness, dirt, smoke, a selection of the countless smells of Glasgow, small, airless, crowded rooms . . . these things make up a picture of the Old College of Glasgow'.

There is now a new College of Glasgow which presents a very different appearance, but, even as things were, the facetious memory of the bun suggests that Lang might have made himself not uncomfortably at home in the old Glasgow College, had time allowed. He got his Snell Exhibition, like his uncle before him, and went to Balliol, where they tried, he somewhere hints, to over-educate him, an attempt which he repelled with ease. An incorrigible habit of reading the classics for what was in them ('philologers and Ireland scholars are not made so'), by debarring him from the chief arena of scholastic triumph, left him freer to find his own. He was of that small, often idle, but wholly legitimate class of students who educate themselves, and find public instruction an uneasy mode of malnutrition. 'It must have been a great privilege, Mr. Lang', said a later admirer, who had been looking up dates, 'for you, a future translator of Homer, to have listened as an undergraduate, at that formative, impressionable period, to Matthew Arnold's famous lectures as Professor of Poetry on Homeric translation.' 'Never heard him', said Lang. 'Undergraduates didn't have to go.' This was certainly a good reason, but a paper of Lang's supplies a better: 'alas, he lectured just at the hour when wickets were pitched on Cowley Marsh'. Lang went his own way, as always: wrote verses, read Greek, played cricket, and talked (a very liberal education), pushed farther from shore on the great ocean of story, and

> rhymed—while the Master read Plato—
> Of Phaeacian men.

It was at or about this time, as he studied the family

likenesses of the folk-tales and mythologies of mankind, that the discovery first dawned upon him which was to occasion his earliest papers on anthropology, and to secure him, as I believe, a permanent place among the historical students of the human mind. He had been interested, even as a boy, to note the recurrence of similar tales among widely distant peoples. He now observed that while these stories differed little in their incidents they differed entirely in their names, and was puzzled to understand how the names, in that case, as it was the fashion to believe, could be the oldest and most significant part of the stories. There had grown up on this assumption, and on others equally unwarranted, an imposing and pretentious school of comparative mythology, of which the high priest in this country was Max Müller: a philological school, which was concerned to derive our folk-tales from the Aryan cradle, and to represent them as the debris of a higher and literary mythology of which the key-words in course of time had been forgotten. The Frog of the fable only talks and goes a-wooing through a linguistic misunderstanding, because in that nobler Aryan civilization the word for Frog once meant the Sun God. Lang was quick to suspect this abracadabra. He suspected it as an undergraduate, and five years later, in a characteristically light but momentous essay, started the chorus of public laughter which was to blow it beyond the moon. He was the first man in this country to see and say plainly that folk-lore is not the debris of a higher mythology, but the foundation on which mythology rests; that anthropology, not philology, is the key to myth; that the clue to its mysteries is to be found not in the cloudland of linguistic conjecture, but in the patient comparative study of the mental habits of primitive man. Primitive man, for example, sees no sort of reason why Frogs should not talk and go a-wooing. Even in the classical mythology, so remote, one had supposed, from savagery, and so glorified by poetry and the idealizing arts, we listen, if we have ears, to the crude ideas of earlier and primitive peoples, blown softly, as Bacon says, through the flutes of Greece.

One other conviction of this youthful and rebellious period should not go unrecorded. He seems to have decided, from a study of savage pictographs, what excavation has since confirmed, that the use and practice of writing is much older than had been estimated. He proceeded to infer that the works of Homer need have depended, for their composition and preservation, on no unique and gigantic feat of memory, but were in all probability committed to writing like the works of other authors. Admire once more the predestination of this undergraduate! Not content with surmising, in the teeth of established opinion, the proper method of studying myths, he had begun his long campaign with the Homeric problem. He felt, like Sir Walter Scott, that the Wolfian hypothesis was worse than wrong, that it was irreligious: a denial of personality, a blasphemy of the Muse. Here, then, was the retort. Prove, for those times, the possibility of literary authorship in its ordinary sense, and Homer steps out the man and the poet that we had instinctively believed him to be. So, in his twenties, Lang argued. He was sapping already, and at their weakest angle, the now crumbled walls of Homeric separatism.

I suppose that the most important practical decision in Lang's life was made when he left Oxford and the learned comforts of a Merton fellowship, and settled in London as a working journalist and man of letters. It was a decision which some of his friends regretted, and there were moments when he regretted it himself. He was walking one night in Merton Street with a younger friend, now an eminent Scottish historian. 'Ah,' he said, 'if I had stayed on here when I was

a young Fellow, and stuck to one thing, I should have
been a big swell by now.' 'Instead of being a big swell
at many things', said his friend. He turned and looked
at him. 'It is very nice of you to say that, and quite
right and proper that you should say it; but you know
it isn't true.' Then, after a pause: 'I should have been
a really big swell at anthropology.' This was in a
moment of gloom; yet it would be idle to deny that we
know what he meant. In no single field—not even in
anthropology, where he valued himself most—did he
ever in fact acquire a position of undisputed domi-
nance. The twinkling goddess of Variety, who taxes
her awards, decreed that he should be brilliant and
originative in all his many subjects, but should be the
Maitland or the Firth of none. I cannot doubt, nevertheless, that he did right to leave Oxford, and that he
was meant for the life he chose: to be a raider, a free-
lance, crossing all men's frontiers. Universities are very
good places in their way, and, if they know their business, erect no barriers between studies; but they are
obliged by mere necessity to a kind of official demarca-
tion which reacts on all concerned. The University
teacher who openly and lavishly studies the subjects of
his colleagues runs the risk of a suspicion that he is
neglecting his own. Lang was not for that world. It
was his destiny in life, while never out of touch with
Universities, to break the fences between specialists,
and to establish understandings, whether cordial or not
(and why not cordial?), between all branches and departments of the humanities. It amuses me to remember the chill air of disapproval with which most of the
classical instructors of my youth regarded his parallels
from anthropology: the identification, for example, of
the ῥόμβος of the Greek mysteries with the Australian
turndun or bull-roarer, and his admission of the prac-
tices of Blackfeet and Maoris to the footnotes of the
Iliad. The suggestion that there could be anything in

common between the minds and customs of such people and the habits of ancient Greece seemed to these gentlemen rather a violation of decency than a contribution to the study of man. I mark those years as an important date in the slow but progressive enlargement of that delicate, somewhat scornful, finely balanced, and undoubtedly important instrument, the classical scholar's mind.

There is a nursery legend that Lang was in the habit, as a child, of arranging six open books on six chairs, and going from one to another perusing them by turns. So early was he proficient in the art of literary *desultura*, and the joy of many things at once. No doubt he diffused himself, but he was almost uniquely tempted: by a range of gifts and interests unequalled in his time, and by a practical facility, a rapidity of composition, astonishing to the hard-bound ring of scholars, and remarkable on occasion even in Fleet Street. I have heard his journalism deplored as a waste of power. Yet of all the professional journalists and essayists of his day he had the most grateful public and kept it longest. It is impossible to assess these things. *Fay ce que voudras* is the motto of the sciences as well as of the arts, and Lang did, more than most men, what he wished. While people were still enumerating the various things he might have been, he strolled about and was them all.

As a scholar his principal motive was curiosity, an emotion, at once rational and romantic, which Dr. Johnson declared to be in generous minds the first passion and the last. It is worth while to observe how instinctively Lang settled, in the studies of his time, on the adventurous, the mysterious, the problematic; on the frontiers of subjects, where new work was being done, and on sciences in the making; Folk-lore and Anthropology, then struggling for recognition and still searching for a method; Ghosts and Dreams, and the

newly organized experiments of Psychical Research;
the old problem of the Ballads; and the vexed question
of Homer. He had early fleshed himself on the classical
mystery of the Iron Mask, the first of an ever-lengthen-
ing series; and had nibbled from youth at the old and
half-gnawed bone of Scottish history. The conditions
of his performance have not always been understood.

'I remember long ago', says W. P. Ker, 'how some people
in Oxford and elsewhere used to speak of Andrew Lang and
wonder if he would ever do anything really great. To those
well-meaning friends and acquaintances he seemed to be
squandering his genius in desultory studies. There were other
persons at the same time who were well enough pleased to read
whatever he wrote on any subject, and did not ask or care
whether he would ever do anything great or not.'

What these friendly but routine critics were looking for
was, as Ker says, one book—big, of course—which
would somehow give the essence of Lang and the full
measure of his powers, and be therefore great. It is
the familiar fallacy of the *magnum opus*. I call it a
fallacy here because the nature of Lang's work demanded the method he employed, an essayist's method,
tentative, skirmishing, reconnoitring, first one book or
paper and then another, keeping the business alive and
always on the move. When a study is in the making,
as so many of Lang's were, a Big Book, a Standard
Book, as we call it, is more likely to be a hindrance than
a help. Large Standard Books, however impressive
and even useful they may be, tend inevitably to arrest
movement. A lively, throbbing, adventurous, explora-
tory study has no right to have Standard Books. Lang,
therefore, wrote none, but went on, instead, simply
clearing the sky and advancing knowledge. He made
no one great discharge, but, like a wise sportsman,
peppered his birds with small shot. When estimating
Lang's services to the studies of his time, do not weigh
the shot, but count the bag. It contained, remarkably

early in his career, the feathers of Max Müller, and of
many other learned gentlemen who did write Standard
Books.

It was a characteristic of Lang, which the plodders
resented, that he could write on nothing like a novice.
Stray as he might, you would have sworn, whatever the
subject, that he had spent his time among its practitioners. Always, in his work, he has this air of his
company, and, whether he writes as a leader or as
a follower, is never confined by his topic to writing
about it merely; he hobnobs and has his joke with it
between times, like a crony. It was remarked by all
who knew him 'how very cheerful' the business of
learning became, or any other business, wherever Lang
was interested. They recalled, when he was dead,
'those sudden letters' that came from him, 'showering
sparks, into the centre of a controversy', and they
thought what they had lost. There was a hilarity in
all his work, a secular blitheness, a harmonious efficacy
of the whole man, extraordinarily refreshing to an age
on which the frown of modern specialism had already
darkened. Lang could be the specialist when he liked.
But he belonged, by right of ancestry, to an earlier,
a simpler, and warmer-hearted tradition. Though his
technique was modern, his temper was of that older
fashion which came to glory in Scott, when literature
and learning, antiquarianism and poetry, the liberal
sciences and arts were still one household, an eager,
unjaded, and romantic partnership. There would
almost seem, in these latter days, to be something
Scottish about it, for which Sir Walter, no doubt, is
responsible. The same glow and generous unity of
mind burns, within a stricter circle, and with a more
sober light, in the work of Lang's friend and fellow-
Sneller, W. P. Ker.

'A mere man of letters', said Samuel Johnson very
truly, 'is a dull man.' To Lang as to Ker the essential

thing was doing. Any man who could *do* anything—
with a rod or a gun, a pen or a sword, it mattered little
which—was a comrade and craftsman to whom he
would gladly dedicate a page. His passion for Causes,
either Lost or so reputed, had its root in deeper things,
but in its executive branches was of a piece with the
rest. For here was action at its brightest: a weapon to
flash, a Maid to defend, a King in exile to be righted
or a God in mufti (whether Homer, the Chevalier, or
the Sminthian Apollo), a fight against odds! Lang was
smiled at, not unkindly, for his enthusiasms, and some
of them, no doubt, were of the mint of old Sir Hilde-
brand. 'The new turnips, and the rats, and the Hano-
verians ha' changed the world that I ha' known.' But
there were others more in trim. It has not sufficiently
been observed how many of Lang's Lost Causes have,
in fact, won. His first victory looks easy now, but no
Cause at that date could well have seemed more
desperate than the explosion of the Sun Myth folly.
The great guns of the Universities boomed its doctrines;
it was embalmed in manuals, and had even begun to
be taught in schools. Lang killed it with a few magazine articles, but he must have seemed at the time
a rash and impudent young man. His darling Cause of
Homeric Unity is the last to triumph. Thirty years
ago it was said that 'no one who has a right to an
opinion now believes in the unity of Homer', and ten
years later 'all scholars' were reported Separatists.
Lang and a few others still went on fighting, and the
Separatists to-day are in open and disgraceful flight. I
could wish that he had lived to see it.

There is one department of Lang's activities at
which I have so far only hinted, congenial as it is to
the occasion of our meeting and to the spirit of this
place: I mean his work in Scottish history. The
subject is dangerous, as he discovered, but he liked
danger, and in an honest quarrel was not afraid of abuse.

Our past, as you know, is volcanic, and from that ancient turbulence strange lava-heaps remain which are molten and treacherous to this day. Highland and Lowland, Jacobite and Whig, Knox and Queen Mary, Argyll and Montrose, the Covenanters and Claver-house, the Archbishop and the holy men of Magus Muir, the Prince and Young Glengarry and the buried treasure of Loch Arkaig—here are problems and anti-theses enough, in an antiquarian and fighting nation, to raise riots. Lang had always been interested, as every Borderer must be, in the ravelled and angry history of his country, but he was over fifty before he found time to take a leading hand. His first venture had been both casual and unfortunate. He wrote a History of St. Andrews, partly because he knew the place, and partly because he was asked to do it, and found himself, in consequence, compelled to pronounce judgement without adequate preparation on some of the thorniest transactions of Scottish history. Out-wardly nothing daunted, he delivered his sentences, expressing with some force rather what he felt than what he knew. The intolerance of the Reformers, who dealt hardly with St. Andrews, received the weight of his arm. 'Here', he wrote, speaking of James Melville, 'here, among the fruits of the Reformation, we have, thank God, a Christian at last.' Flowers of this kind make an uneasy wreath, and Lang was furiously answered. The Scot, it has been said, is not a quarrel-some man, but has a fine sense of the value of provoca-tion; and so it was here. Lang was not wilfully com-bative. But it did so happen, in the course of a busy life, that most of the subjects which he took up were controversial. He was accused of deliberate insult to his country, and was taunted, not for the last time, as a renegade Scot.

The clamour, I think, surprised him; he had not expected that the bodies of the Reformers had so much blood in them. But what touched him more was the exposure of his errors: the discovery, as he confessed, 'that he did not know the rules of the game'. These rules he was soon to learn. His friend Robert Louis Stevenson (he tells the story himself) had begged for Jacobite material to be used in a novel, and Lang, who helped everybody, and would do anything for Stevenson, went digging for Jacobite novelties in the Pelham Papers. He found a mine of mystery, and transcripts were duly sent out to Samoa, though too late to be of much use. This was in 1893; Stevenson died the following year; and the papers were returned. What was he to do with them? His first thought as a man of letters was to make a novel of them, a kind of Jacobite *Barry Lyndon*, with Young Glengarry, the discovered traitor, as the gentleman villain. Instead he wrote, and presently published, *Pickle the Spy*. It had been an exciting but unpleasant task, and the reception of the book was such as must have been foreseen. Once more a storm of indignation whistled about his ears, this time from over the Highland hills. Even for a Scottish historian it was a rough beginning. With two books, in four years, he had raised the fighting remnants of all Scotland, and had incurred the equal execration of the descendants of the Reformers and of the Highland cavaliers. This time, however, he had made no mistake. *Pickle* was based on a thorough study of sources. He now gave the advice, 'Always go to the MSS.', and from the year of his illumination he always did so himself. To this passion for historicity, indeed, for getting the thing 'richt as it was', he came near, in the end, to sacrificing the last possession a man of letters parts with, his sense of literary form. What should have been essays swelled into books, and what was meant to be narrative became inquiry. I have no wish to commend his example in this matter. But it is worth remarking in a man whom duller historians have been known to

describe as a merely literary person. It may even excite
some curiosity in an age when historical fact is by
so many of our younger writers openly subjugated to
style.

For ten years after *Pickle* Scottish history became
one of Lang's principal occupations, and he left in that
time a permanent mark on the study. Perhaps the
greatest praise that can be given to him is that, in one
of the most highly romanced and most partisan fields
of human story, he, a romancer and avowed partisan,
is never content with legend and is never unfair. I
should have liked, if time allowed, to substantiate that
statement, but the evidence is public. He never shirks
unpopular judgements: exposes the shiftiness of the
young de Bruce, the treacheries of the great House of
Douglas, so often neither 'tender' nor 'true', the guilt
(though it wrings his heart to do it) of Mary Queen of
Scots, and the shady side of his own Jacobite cause.
The same candour and evenness of hand distinguish
his account of our relations with England. He takes
a patriot's pleasure in the old campaigns of independence, the heroic days, but he reports the jarring
notes in our often discordant song of freedom. Few, it
would seem, of our medieval ancestors thought twice
of breaking an oath. They constantly broke faith with
one another, and with equal assiduity perjured themselves to England. Wishart, Bishop of Glasgow, was
a sterling patriot; he was also, by the same token, the
most accomplished perjurer of his age. 'Swearing was
then, as it were, a matter of magic. A man chose the
one saint, or relic, or formula that would bind him—
and kept it a profound secret. Other oaths he took with
a light heart.' Edward I could never discover which
the right oaths were. So Lang proceeds, mixing truth
and fun in his habitual manner. Yet he fights the case
of Scotland inch by inch against the English claims, and
stands no nonsense from Mr. Freeman.

His opinion of the Reformers and Covenanters he seems never to have changed, though he improved his evidence. 'Our modern freedom of thought and belief is the inestimable heritage of the Reformation, but it is a heritage which neither Reformer nor Covenanter intended to bequeath.' The county of Fife was of the stiff-necked party in those days, and talked 'the patois of Canaan', but he forgives it for your sake. I observe that he always brightens up, in his *History of Scotland*, when St. Andrews is named: 'this pugnacious University.' Even of Argyll (Gillespie Gruamach), who burned the Bonnie House of Airlie and was the enemy of the great Montrose, he thinks noticeably better because he was once a student here, and approved of golf.

One of the severest tests of a Scottish historian is his attitude to that romance of the Highlands which, real as it is, the works of Scott and the tourist agencies have to some extent imposed upon us. I confess that on this matter, from some fault or virtue of the blood, I cannot think impartially. When tartan falls out with broadcloth I fall in with tartan. Lang is more composed, and, though it costs him something, steadily resists the Celtic glamour. 'The civilization of Scotland', he repeatedly declares, 'depended, and has always depended, on the predominance of the English element over the Celtic . . . , to take an extreme instance, of Bailie Nicol Jarvie over Rob Roy.' In the Celt, he goes so far as to suggest, along with that singular fatality which has dogged his race, there is to be found a certain nimiety, a kind of bragging incompetence; and he recalls the 'four-and-twenty men' with 'five-and-thirty pipers' who accompanied a well-known chief on a well-known fatal expedition. The Celts, he evidently believes, in their romantic progress through history, have been always over-orchestraed. Even the far-famed 'Celtic note' sheds much of its mystery in his pages, and

something also of its patent rights; for, offend whom
he may, he cannot forget his anthropology. The
'Celtic note', it would appear, is no more Celtic than
it is Finnish, being the result 'not of race, but of an
isolated life in lonely forests or hills, a life led by a dis-
possessed and unsuccessful people'. Of all poetry,
indeed, 'that of the Australian natives is most akin to
the Celtic'.

We shall spear Borrah on the morillas,
And Dinewan shall fall when we throw.
But Eerin will hunt with us no longer,
Never again will Eerin eat of our hunting.
Hunt shall we often, and oft shall we find,
But the widow of Eerin will kindle no fires for his coming.

Where were these verses made? In Ireland or Albin?
This 'Celtic' snatch from the Antipodes gave little
pleasure, I should suppose, in the halls and manses of
Caledonia, for there are finds which please only their
discoverers. Yet he laments the Celtic fate as he adores
the Highland virtues, and he regards with a distaste
that might satisfy even 'the indignant spirit of the
North' that dreary process of substitution by which
'English brewers, soap-boilers, and upholsterers sit in
the seats of Macdonnells and Macphersons'.

You would have a right to complain if I said nothing
in this lecture about Lang's verse. Different judgements have been passed upon it, but oddly, and I am
sure unfortunately, the harshest judgement was his
own. He was a man to whom verse-making was as
natural as breathing and very nearly as easy, and perhaps for that reason was suspicious of his gifts. In his
later years he would bluntly deny that his rhymes were
poetry at all. Some of you may remember the warm
and generous little Preface which he wrote, a few years
before his death, to Charles Murray's *Hamewith*. It
contains, in all soberness apparently, these astonishing
words—'were I a poet'. I can understand his getting

tired, and others with him, of the frail and rather
throatless music of his charming rondeaux and ballades,
though some of these will live. It is intelligible that
his Swinburnian dexterities should cease to please. A
deafness to those tunes has been growing upon us for
a generation. But when all deductions are made, when
we have allowed for satiety and the innocent fickleness
of the human ear, how rich in good things are the
verses of this spendthrift poet! Lang lost as well as
gained by his period. Growing up, as he did, in the
purple age of Victorian poetry, when Tennyson and
Swinburne were the gods of verse, he felt his genius
rebuked, and, having made his effort, retired too readily
from the greater game. It all goes back, I believe, to
Helen. The six books of this poem were his diploma
piece, his one laborious bid for honours, and he took
their failure too much to heart. Now *Helen* is a Sleep-
ing Beauty that was never awake. He spoke freely from
this time, though never, I think, with bitterness, of
'the peaks forbidden', and of himself as the strolling
musician of Parnassus.

> I, too, to please my Saintsbury,
>   The barrel-organ will essay,
>   Once more my penny-whistle ply,
>   Be archly sad, or glumly gay.

The greater instruments, the deeper tones, were not
for him. He may have been right, and of course he
had other things to do; but what was wrong was the
discouragement. 'I have always thought his verse in-
conceivably underrated', says Mr. Saintsbury. 'Did
he ever know', asks another friend, 'how much his
poetry was admired?' I am afraid he never did. His
nimbler talent, always certain of a welcome, showered
its quizzical delights. But his quiet poems of romance,
his songs of the affections, partly, no doubt, because
he seemed to slight them himself, have in fact been
slighted. Here in St. Andrews, where his eastland

verses are on every lip, you run less danger of this ingratitude. Nor is it likely that his native Borders,
pampered as they have been with song and fable, will
forget the loyal and wistful Muse of Andrew Lang.

It is odd that he should ever have been accused of
Anglicizing.

'To speak for myself', he says, 'I am never so happy as when
I cross the Tweed at Berwick from the South, or go on the links
at Wimbledon, to hear the accents (for there are several, in-
cluding that peculiar to Gourock) of my native tongue. These
observes are quite genuine, and come from a Scot whose critics
in England banter him on his patriotism, while his critics in
Scotland revile him as rather more unpatriotic than the in-
famous Sir John Menteith, who whummled the bannock.'

Such are the penalties, to a Scot, of historical impartiality in damning conjunction with a London residence!
But these things are past, and Scotland does well to
honour Lang's memory. No man of his time understood or loved her better, or took, in England, a more
ironic pleasure in being a Scot. The old game of North
and South was a perpetual refreshment to him, though
it must have seemed sometimes the driest of jokes
that he should be writing for Southrons in London
when he might be fishing in the Esk or reading Pits-
cottie in St. Andrews. Through all his writing, and
especially his later writing, there runs this gentle irony
of the exile, like his favourite Dalgetty serving his
foreign master faithfully, but reserving always the
right to remember Drumthwacket and the humanities
of Marischal College. Lang was in the old Scots
tradition. He was of the old race, one of the family of
Sir Walter, and proud that the world should know it.
Had Edinburgh remained what Edinburgh once was, a
metropolis of letters, he need never have gone South.

You are probably aware that there will be no official
Life of Lang, or collection of his Letters. That was
his wish, and his wish must be respected. I cannot help

feeling sorry. The usual result of such embargoes may
be seen in the fate of Thackeray. He left a similar
injunction, and the consequence is that he is still imperfectly understood, because only bad or indifferent
Lives of him could be written. A Life of Lang even
half as good as his own Life of Lockhart would have
been something worth having. As it is, we must be
content, for the time, with the occasional reminiscences
of friends, and with the brief account of him just
published in the *Dictionary of National Biography*. For
that account I am myself responsible, and I have considered it as relieving me, in this lecture, from some
biographical duties, and from the more ordered consideration of his works. I believe it to be accurate
except in one particular. The six months which I have
allowed for his book on Joan of Arc, written in answer
to the higher cynicism of Anatole France, Mrs. Lang
now tells me were nearer three. I had thought six
a short allowance, yet in a fourth of that time, I can
fancy him remarking, Sir Walter wrote *Guy Mannering*.

Lang's fear of an official or family biography was
partly due, no doubt, to a dislike of that kind of book.
He had seen, as we all have, so many painful examples
of it, and he had been, as an author, in the kitchen
where these things are cooked. If all sons-in-law were
Lockharts, and all nephews Trevelyans, the case would
be altered. But the principal deterrent was Lang himself. He was a shy man, though offended strangers
might not at first observe this, for he had the shy man's
outworks. It was his habit to conceal behind an air of
detachment, or a mask of gruffness, not only a most
generous and active benevolence, but a spirit only less
sensitive than that of Lockhart himself. What Scott
noted of Lockhart, the shyest of men—his 'reserve,
and a sort of Hidalgo air', and a way of seeming to quiz
the company from a corner—might be transferred
direct to Lang. Even his prodigious industry, his

'absolutely regardless' fashion of working on any question he took up, was carefully screened from observation. To stay with him at his house in St. Andrews was to believe that he had nothing to do but play golf and talk, being, I understand, though it is not for me to speak, more dexterous at the second than at the first. It is in the same line of character that, in spite of many importunities, he should have had his portrait painted only once, though he was not equally successful in escaping the blunter addresses of the camera. The portrait was painted in 1887 by Sir William Richmond, when Lang was forty-three, and I am glad to be able to state, on the authority of Mrs. Lang, that its ultimate destination is the Scottish National Portrait Gallery. He is needed there to complete, with Stevenson—'dear Andrew' and 'dear Louis' together—the honourable succession of the House of Scott.

X

WALTER RALEIGH IN HIS LETTERS[1]

WHEN Sir Walter Raleigh died, now nearly four
years ago, and his friends one after another tried
their hands at describing him, some professional ap-
praisers of genius thought it proper to be sceptical.
Had we really lost, and had they missed, by not knowing
him, so much? Or was this only another of those
charming personalities which blow in, by the grace of
God, with every generation, and by the judgement of
Adam go out with it: a passing colour and warmth
of humanity, grateful but evanescent? The pictures
drawn of him were thought by some to support this
view. They were accused of being all tints and no
anatomy, like the pictures of —— or the criticism of
——. There was talk of a 'Raleigh legend'. That
such a legend existed it would be idle to deny. He
lived much among the young, and the young, who must
worship somebody, chose to worship him. He had
many friends, who with unfailing relish and varying
success would repeat his sayings. But the point would
seem to be that the legend has refused to fade, and is
rapidly approaching what is more commonly called
fame. It is on the way to be history, and these Letters,
so much talked of, are its documents. There was similarly an Elia legend, and Carlyle, from the outside, was
similarly sceptical. He resembled some of the gentlemen I think of in his jealousy of the illusions of others,
and in his willingness to make the world a desert for the
pleasure of preaching in the wilderness. The answer to
both scepticisms is a bundle of correspondence.

[1] Revised and reprinted from an article in *The London Mercury*,
vol. xiii, April 1926, reviewing *The Letters of Sir Walter Raleigh*,
1879–1922, edited by Lady Raleigh and published by Methuen.

Raleigh's letters are of the right sort for this purpose. They are the nearest thing possible to speech, to the man talking, and almost none of them was written for the purpose of being overheard. The illusion, indeed, in the later letters especially, is overpowering. I felt, said the Poet Laureate, after reading some hundred pages of them, as if he had been sitting talking there, and it was growing late, and time he went home across the fields. It is doubtful if it ever occurred to him that his letters were kept. So far was he from saving his good things, or providing for their preservation, that he did not even remember them. 'Did I say that? I daresay it may be true.' 'That's the worst of it', he writes, when reminded of something, 'I never remember what I say. "Plenty more where that came from" *was* my line. So it will be rather desolate and wilted when there isn't plenty more, and I haven't saved up what there was. But I daresay I shall die before I'm reduced to tinned provisions.' He thought that when one remembered *things said*, in the Holland House manner, it meant that 'the talk had lumps in it and did not go with a rush. The very few times in my life that I have calmly and purposefully said "a good thing", I have always felt like an undertaker bringing in the body.' Talk should be struck out at the moment, enjoyed, and thrown aside. His later friend and master, Samuel Johnson, knew this well, but was less enlightened when it came to letters, making it positively an objection that a letter is addressed to a single mind 'the prejudices and partialities of which are known to the writer'. Raleigh noted this as evidence that Johnson, with all his power and tenderness, seemed not cut out for letter-writing: epistolography was another matter. His own letters, like his conversation, address themselves instinctively, without afterthought or safeguard, to the friend and the occasion. He had many anonymous friends, and concealed admirers, one of them his wine-merchant, and perhaps the sincerest compliment ever paid to a letter-writer was paid to Raleigh from his office. It was not that the orders placed were large or particularly choice. Here I am, says Raleigh in 1911, just knighted, and 'wondering if it would be a good day to open a bottle of cheap claret'. But his wine-merchant, writing to Lady Raleigh after his death, confessed with some searching of conscience, and with apologies for the loss of time it might have caused him, that they had sometimes concocted unnecessary business letters to him for the sole purpose of receiving his replies.

How much survives of a man who put talk first, letters second, and books a long way after both, must always be to some extent a matter of luck. Raleigh endured no Boswell, and if over 2,000 of his letters have been preserved, it is because his correspondents thought them worth preserving. There have been losses of course. His letters to R. A. M. Stevenson and Henley would have been worth seeing; and I recall, at a later date, a minor loss, some letters to myself, as vivid as almost any in these volumes, which disappeared with some baggage I could better spare, in the war in France. I remember how they cheered our mess, who had almost come to believe that no civilian was capable of the truth, and how I had to describe him, and how we drank his health. There are letters here that would have delighted them, as, On Looking up a Neutral:

'All right, I'll look the Johnny up. I confess the company of intelligent conversational neutrals makes me sick, but I'll look him up. They ask you how you feel about the war, and whether you think that Fletcher or B. Jonson was the stronger "factor" in influencing Shirley, who, of course, would never have written a line if he had not been "influenced" by his mother and his nurse and everyone else. But I'll look him up, and I'll try to pretend it's all right. What's he doing here? Reading in libraries, I suppose, and forming aesthetic judgments. By

God! I'll look him up. It'll be all right. They're starting a munitions factory here, and if he isn't working in it pretty soon, I'll look him up several times. So don't you worry; I'm glad you mentioned him.'

He says somewhere, of Lord Balfour, 'I don't believe he'll make a letter-writer; he gets to the point at once, and then stops'. He, on the contrary, belonged to 'the garrulous crew'. But some of his letters answer the curb as well as Lord Balfour's. His reply, in December 1914, to a letter from Sir Hall Caine, about 'a literary album, all gush and rant, to be given to the King of the Belgians', is Wellingtonian in its dispatch:

Dear Sir,
The best present to give to the King of the Belgians is Belgium. Two of the men of this household are at the front, and the third is drilling.

Yours truly,
W. A. RALEIGH.

This letter is accidentally preserved in the text of another. It was inspired not only by the obvious irrelevance of the proposal, but by a contempt, which had long been gathering in Raleigh, for the fuss and vanity of authors. The war tried them, it appears. Speech 'went down in price'. They felt, he says, that they didn't matter, and they couldn't bear it: 'like the men of the Basque nation who take to their beds and receive congratulations when their wives have a child.'

Raleigh, in his published writings, seldom spoke of himself, so that these letters are the more welcome. They range in time from his eighteenth year to a few days before his death, and are all that is claimed for them: the best kind of biography, and in the first rank of their kind. Sir Edmund Gosse, in an interesting and reminiscent notice, has emphasized the importance of Raleigh's undergraduate time at Cambridge, and regrets that in the collected Letters there is so little from that period. I should like to put in a word, if 'influence' is the cry, for his earlier and still less recorded undergraduate experiences in London, and to quote from *England and the War* his account of the 'indescribable exhilaration' with which he entered University College, and made the acquaintance of teachers 'who cared much about their subject and little or nothing about their pupils':

'To escape from the eternal personal judgments which make a school a place of torment is to walk upon air. The schoolmaster looks at you; the college professor looks the way you are looking. The statements made by Euclid, that thoughtful Greek, are no longer encumbered at college with all those preposterous and irrelevant moral considerations which desolate the atmosphere of a school. The question now is not whether you have perfectly acquainted yourself with what Euclid said, but whether what he said is true.'

Here is Raleigh's life-long creed of the business of a university, fought for in Liverpool, in Glasgow, and in Oxford, and exemplified with such careless magnanimity in his own practice. I should say that University College, London, had a good deal more to do with it than Cambridge, which must have seemed to him, with its tutorial anxieties, in some respects a retrogression, a return to school. As late as 1917 he remembered University College as 'a place of delight', because he found there 'the delights of freedom'.

Cambridge gave him other things: a community to live with, and a haunted place to dream in. He read to the 'Owls' on *Romeo and Juliet*, he was an 'Apostle', and President of the Union, acted 'Macready's part' in *Money*, edited the *Cambridge Review*, and played golf for Cambridge against Oxford. I note one odd thing. He talks much about music in his Cambridge letters, and had many musical friends, but from the age of 25 music is never again mentioned in his correspondence, nor did I ever hear him speak of it. But then

I had known him for years without suspecting his addiction to chess-problems.

He said, at the end of his life, that he would rather have missed Cambridge than India. He was there two years from 24 to 26; it gave him horizon, and what he liked to call 'the wide world'. He discovered missionaries, and concluded that 'evangelical magic is as harmful as any other superstition'. He found that in India, 'where you see all the bones of the Leviathan', Sidgwick's well-known treatise on Politics is 'unreal, vaporous, pedantic, pettifogging, and meaningless'. He found out Macaulay, and marked with enlightened eyes the effect of Burke upon the Eastern mind. It was a lesson he never forgot. 'The art of writing', he told his Oxford students,

'cannot be learnt by a close study of Burke's rhetoric. The flowers and fruits of style grow on the tree of character. The attempt to imitate Burke has nevertheless been made. One whole nation, the Bengalis, mimic his speech. The effect is exactly like what may sometimes be seen in the branches of the trees of an Indian forest—the monkeys are behaving in a strange and unnatural manner, a manner that is unintelligible until the cause is discovered. A man has passed that way.'

He always meant to write; the question was, how he should live by it. There was a project of living on porridge and scones in a Yorkshire cottage on £100 per annum—a kind of Craigenputtock; and when he returned from India, there was a little journalism in London. But he was fated to be a Professor, and soon found himself in Manchester, 'this exceedingly nasty city', lecturing 'in a very picaroon, jolly beggar kind of way', though really almost killed by it. 'For all fair and humane influences I might as well be down a sewer.' At Liverpool he was happier, though words, once more, 'could not convey an idea of the people' there; even five years later, 'commercial Liverpool' was still beyond him. These references, duly indexed, and

some others to Glasgow, will not be much loved in the
North; but they should not be taken too seriously. It
was in Liverpool and Glasgow that Raleigh learned to
know and to like business men: he liked them, he said,
'because they didn't fuss', like dons and authors. But
that was on their own ground. On his, the shoe
creaked, it was another matter, and he saw them only
as 'solid level-headed Protestants, pounding away at
culture'. But he was very cheerful in Liverpool,
feathering his nest with artists and other 'restful
things', and from one of them, R. A. M. Stevenson,
learning more than from any single person he ever met.
In Stevenson he found that unprofessionalism he so
much admired and so admirably practised: 'it was the
incomparable charm of R. A. M. Stevenson that his
real life began where his job ended . . . so he escaped the
curse of the actor, preacher, the writer, the professor,
and remained a private gentleman.'

Raleigh came to his maturity at Glasgow, where he
resumed at 39 his study of the Scot, and changed, says
Mr. Phillimore, the whole temper of the intellectual
life of the University. It is perhaps too much to hope
that his views on Education, on the Dull Student, and
on Universities as places where young men go to choose,
will ever wholly commend themselves to the pedagogic
community. The nursing instinct is too strong. He
had early come to the conclusion that character is
formed sooner than is commonly supposed, and never
saw much reason to alter his conviction that 'a man
who cannot take care of himself at 21 is always best
drowned'. They told me in Liverpool, he says, that it was

'all-important to spend many hours on diminishing the in-
capacity of dull students. I did not contradict them, but I
didn't do it: I wrote a book. No one who understands the real
thing cares twopence about the dull student, except as a man
and a brother. Drink with him, pray with him; don't read with
him, except for money.'

His subject troubled him: 'everyone rightly thinks that he can read English literature for himself, and that no lecturer is needed.' His audiences would not have agreed with him, but his opinion held. 'If I am accused on Judgment Day of teaching literature', he wrote to me, 'I shall plead that I never believed in it and that I maintained a wife and children. I don't know what old Bradley and G. Murray will plead, but I long to hear.' The annual yoking of the poets to the academic curriculum was an operation always painful to him, and more painful the more conscientiously it was performed.

'The theories of women tutors about the *sequence* of classes are beyond finding out. They ticket Chaucer as elementary; Shakespeare, I believe, is advanced. The text, in the books they use (which always have notes) comes first; so it's elementary. All the English poets stand, like bright-harnessed angels, in order serviceable, ready to perform their assigned work, and to prepare the virgin's mind for examination.'

This was probably never quite a fair account, but it is near enough the awful truth. It is the machine that does it: the examination of which every college tutor, male or female, is perforce a 'minder'. Sometimes he breaks out at Universities altogether: 'no sense in them . . . bottled men.'

He became early disaffected to literary criticism, and though he played it so well, thought it a poor game. 'I ought to have written straight—on things. Now I can't acquire the art.' The eunuch, he is persuaded, was the first modern critic. ' "Understandest thou what thou readest?" said Philip. The eunuch was then baptized (they all are) and served him right. And the business of literary criticism began.' He came more and more to feel that 'critical admiration for what another man has written is an emotion for spinsters'.

'Jerome K. Jerome is in some ways a far decenter writer than Brunetière or Saintsbury or any of the professed critics.

He goes and begets a brat for himself, and doesn't pule about other people's amours. If I write an autobiography it shall be called "Confessions of a Pimp".'

Raleigh is enjoying himself, for he is writing to John Sampson; but he meant most of it; though if critics live on authors, I cannot quite see why it should not be permitted to them to discuss their food. His book on 'The Habits of the Human Race' was never written 'straight', but most of it was published for all that, having inserted itself obliquely while he wrote of other things. Life slips in easily when the theme is Shakespeare or Johnson or Robert Burns; and there was the Epic of England to come. He had his say after all.

He was often called 'flippant', and no reader of these letters need be told why. Church, and State, and the Education bogey he tested by the same rules as one applies to daily things. His letter *On an Old Friend who thought of taking Orders* will offend some readers, though none, perhaps, who is capable of reading Shakespeare; but if they call it 'flippant', we have a right to see their bumps.

'Tell P. I don't mind his being systematic, but I'm damned if I could know him after he takes orders. I have forgiven orders to the young and foolish before now (though of course to take orders advertises that you don't want your friends to say what they think in your presence). Tell P. he's not a religious man. *This I know*, it's not an opinion. Tell him to come (not go) to Hell, along with a set of decent coves. Tell him not to go blacklegging it along with the spiritual police.

'I won't see P. after he takes orders. I'm willing enough, but I couldn't. You can't help a gentleman who's found salvation. And by God, he can't help you. But I should like to dine with him before we part for this world and the next. . . .

'I'm told there's a funny little separate Hell for those who take orders for wrong reasons. It's not a tragic Hell (as the clergy suppose), it's a comic little Hell where everyone to all eternity makes jokes that don't come off.'

This may be all a very lamentable mistake, but it

answers uncommonly to his own definition of Humour:
'thinking in fun while feeling in earnest.' In real life,
when Raleigh's gipsyisms perturbed his company, it
was as often as not a matter of pace. I have seen so
many of those four-wheeled vehicles toiling in vain
after his go-cart. He loved fun and banter, and hated
explaining, but there is little in these letters that has
not experience behind it. I am reminded of a story of
Cowper's which he liked. 'I remember', says Cowper,
'that Samuel Cox the counsel, walking by the sea-side
as if absorbed in deep contemplation, was questioned
about what he was musing on. He replied: "I was
wondering that such an almost infinite and unwieldy
element should produce a sprat." ' The observation,
he would say, might serve as a parable to explain
Cowper's humour, and, I would add, his own fun. 'His
sprats were the harvest of the deep.'

Raleigh called himself a Scot, but was of mixed
blood—Scots, Irish, and English. The mixture gave
him, he claimed, a certain detachment and authority
when he discussed, as he loved to do, the inhabitants of
these islands, and especially the central fact of the
English character. His astonishing letter on the Scottish nation, written in his first months at Glasgow,
might so easily escape attention in this country, and is
so little likely to be proclaimed in the country to which
it refers, that I feel it my duty, however wounded by
its darts, to quote it here:

'I see you don't know the Scots. They are a superstitious,
loyal, useful, jealous, impossible people. A long course of their
own theology has hopelessly perverted their attitude. I know
Scots who are modest—modest towards men; I don't know a
single Scot who is modest on behalf of man. They have the
name of philosophy, but there is more philosophy in a Berkshire
peasant than in all their professors. If they succeed—and they
are always struggling and asserting themselves—it is a great
thing; if they fail, so do heroes, and it is still a great thing.

Rhetoric has poxed them to the bone. They will die with courage in the last ditch, but it must be the last—a remarkable ditch. Merely to die in a ditch is beyond them. . . . It is impossible not to esteem them, and they are the best friends— if you have fish to fry. If you are doing nothing in particular, they leave you, for they must be getting on. Since I lived in Scotland I can't think of Charles Lamb without the tears coming to my eyes—tears like those that are wept by an over-wrought spirit who dreams of rest. To have no particular object in life, but to take it as it comes—you will find this in China, in India, in France, in England; I have not found it in Scotland. . . .

'They will ruin me, for although they are ready to believe in aggressive eccentricity (as of a prophet) they will have nothing to say to idle whim. A gospel is your passport in Scotland.'

There is more truth in this account than is comfortable, but a Scot, I hope, can stand the truth. It should be read along with his later study in the Essay on Burns. Lord Charles Beresford, as one of these letters discloses, took Raleigh for an Irishman, characteristically thanking God for it, and a merry conspiracy has been started to uphold Lord Charles, and explain Raleigh by Ireland. He was certainly attracted to the Irish, and would even defend their habits. 'I always liked the Irish best.' 'I am awfully comfortable among them. Ireland is a perfect nest for all that is most profoundly unsatisfactory in my temper and character. So I love the Irish.' Their lack of worldly success he explained to their credit. 'I don't see how Ireland can ever be prosperous, it is too human.' In the war he still thought kindly of them. 'Lucie says all the Irish are knaves. I think (being old and tolerant) that they are luxuries; and like other luxuries are sometimes more useful than necessaries.' Can the speculative genealogists be right? To Mr. Phillimore the picture presented by these letters is the gradual disengaging of an inner Irishman from a shell of Scottish inhibitions.

'You could not see his grey eye or hear his talk without

speculating on an equation Raleigh—Rahilly at some point in his ancestry. The wit that was, as he liked to assert, "another method of thinking", the fancy that abounded in grotesque drollery of imagery, the humour that in him conditioned such deep and sympathetic insight into character and moods: these were Irish traits. So was the uproarious fooling, the ridicule of pose and importance. . . . He got more Irish as he grew older.'

His family was of Kirkcudbrightshire, which gives these guesses a more engaging likelihood, and on the heels of Mr. Phillimore's conjecture comes a letter from a cousin to say that in their common grandfather's Family Bible it is recorded that they came from Ireland. So, it is also recorded, did Christianity. It would have amused Raleigh, this research.

The time has perhaps hardly come to ask what his place will be among the men of letters of his day, and where he stands among the critics; but Oxford is already encouraging answers to the question. The place of Sir Walter Raleigh among Literary Critics has just been announced as the subject of a University Prize Essay. It is impossible to predict what the judgement of the youngsters will be; but if they compare him, as they are not unlikely to do, with Matthew Arnold, the results should be interesting. Raleigh's essay on Arnold as a critic is one of his best performances, and stands out from the rest of his critical work by a bitterness of tone which surprised himself. 'An odd thing happened to it. It came out much more hostile than I intended or knew I thought.' It is an essay on the weaknesses of the cosmopolitan spirit when applied to nations and their literature; it is, in other words, 'an essay on the cultured Jew'. His occupation just before with the writings of such an Englishman in grain as the first Lord Halifax ('the delight to find John Bull a wit!') may account, perhaps, for some of the hostility and some of the surprise. Arnold had a wider grasp of literature than Raleigh, but a smaller

grasp of life, and they aim at different marks. Raleigh's
game is always the Man rather than the Book, and he
hunts with the perceptions of a woodsman. Arnold
never hunts, or hardly ever. He fires at ascertained
ranges, like a Bisley shot.

There is an unpublished letter of Raleigh's written
in 1908 to the Clarendon Press when he was thinking
of his *Halifax*, which gives, with some raciness, his
later creed.

'From his [Lord Halifax's] time to the time of his grandson,
Chesterfield, cold-drawn truth was obtainable at the English
tap. Then Romance was turned on again, and everything
became luscious and exalted. Halifax no doubt was then
thought *low*; but there's no affection among the Romantics like
the affection of the *Advice to a Daughter*. Shelley was fond of
no one; Keats loved a Cockney minx; Wordsworth viewed with
eye serene the very pulse of a machine. Halifax was simply
fond of his daughter, and anxious to help her in a difficult
world.'

This is a far cry from his first tastes in literature, as these
Letters show; and the gradual change of these tastes and
the formation of his settled literary judgement await, no
doubt, the thesis-writers of the future. It is a movement, slow at first and casual, but then made in a
bound, from Romanticism to the Fact: from the hag-
gard swooning art of the Romantics to the cooler
methods of another day: from the Romantic view of
life to Samuel Johnson's. He was, at 20, one of the
first of the Browningites, deserted Browning at 27
('fubsy old Browning') for Rossetti and his diviner
sister, and never took to him again. 'I don't really care
for Browning,' he writes in 1905, 'I think it "homely"
(as the Americans say) to keep on talking so much
about the soul.' Burns, Keats, Shelley, are his gods for
a time, and he becomes a Meredithian (but only for
his verse). As to Pope, he cannot, in 1889, conceive
'how a definition of poetry that is not a much better

definition of almost anything else could be invented to include his works'. In 1890 he is revelling in Chaucer ('when one has read him for a few weeks one cares for little else'), and is 'a swell on W.S.'s Sonnets from long poring'. He has found out the Elizabethans, and draws, characteristically, a perverted worldly pleasure even from Stubbes the Puritan's *Anatomy of Abuses*. 'Every fresh abuse—such as May-games, Morris Dances, nights in the woods—makes one's mouth water.' He studies Milton, and hopes, with some warrant, that his book on that poet may have 'ended the career of the pietistic old gentleman of scholarly habits who wrote works good for Sunday afternoon reading, and restored the blazing and acrid visionary'. He seems never at any time to have liked Thackeray, or Meredith either, except in his poems, or the melioristic George Eliot. He wished instead for 'a Trollope movement—it would be so healthy'. Wordsworth steadied him, but never became a part of his mind as Shakespeare did. He was conscious of Shakespeare's eye on him while he was writing; 'I don't want to write anything that William Himself would have thought rot'; but he did not care in the least what Wordsworth thought of his *Wordsworth*.

I take it to have been about the year 1902 or 1903 that the Romanticism of the nineteenth century began noticeably to gibber as he looked at it, and I ascribe at any rate the decisiveness of the change to his discovery of Samuel Johnson. It was a late discovery, as he subsequently lamented; for Macaulay and the Romantics had deceived him about the Doctor:

'You are lucky to find Johnson out before you are old, or indeed at all [he wrote in 1918]. God help me, I had to lecture on him before I knew him, and poked fun at him all the time, at second hand. . . . I can't remember how I escaped. I think I came across remarks like that on Tom Thumb, and realised that it didn't fit. . . . Now I think I like him best. Nothing is too good to say about him. The things he hasn't got don't matter.'

The magnitude of this change may be estimated by comparing what he says of *The Rambler* in his *English Novel* of 1894 and in his 1907 Leslie Stephen lecture. He first strongly suspected, I fancy, that all was not well with the Romantic case or at any rate with Romantic criticism, when he discovered what it had thrown aside: Johnson's Essay on Shakespeare, for example, which he was recommending to his classes, in terms apparently extravagant, about the year 1901. By 1904, when he moved to Oxford, he was busy with a course of lectures on the Romanticism of the Nineteenth Century—'the purpose mainly anti-Romantic' —which was to contain his creed, up to date. It was 'the Classic creed, with trimmings', and at this trial of the Romantics only Wordsworth was acquitted. Two years later the great Moralist has become a standing test, and a public lecture of the time is dismissed from commendation as in its style 'almost dangerously unlike the writing or speech of Samuel Johnson'. In 1907 he was lecturing on Johnson at Cambridge, and in 1908 appeared his *Johnson on Shakespeare*.

'As a work of piety I've collected all the best of the old man's notes on Shakespeare. . . . I love it: hardly any one else will. . . . I felt bound to do something about Johnson. People can't understand that one should love him. . . . Boswell's not quite guiltless. His aloofness has made Johnson a *curiosity*. No critic speaks of him as a friend. It's monstrous.'

His *Six Essays*, two years later, summed up his Johnsonian message to the age, and more than any other single book inaugurated the present triumph of Johnson, and the revaluation, now proceeding, of the eighteenth century. Whether he would have relished some recent excesses of the cult—Johnson services in St. Clement Danes, and the almost Stratfordian veneration for his relics—may be confidently doubted. 'How much better London is now that people walk about the streets to look at them. . . . What does it matter where Dr. Johnson lived?'

There were rebels, of course, and there are rebels, noble rebels, still:

'R. Bridges says he [Johnson] was a one-eyed man. But then so many of the two-eyed men, like —— and —— and Ruskin, though they enjoy the use of a fine rolling liquid orb for romantic and poetic purposes, in addition to the little pig eye that we all use at home,—so many of them, I say, are martyrs to miasma. With old Johnson you get away from medicine bottles, and fans, and mew-cat artificial voices, and spiritual affinities. And the little pig eye does wonderful work. It's a pity that so many of the two-eyed men are minxes.'

Raleigh could not help feeling, as he reached middle life, that the Romantics, and Romanticism, were just a little silly. W. Morris was 'just a little silly', and 'everyone who writes about him is just a little silly, too'. Shelley goes silly: 'we have a great many silly men (like Shelley) who could never have kept alive if women had been equally silly.' It is the distinction, on the contrary, of Halifax (as of Johnson) that he is 'never silly', and he doubts, in 1912, if the new age is fit to read him.

So we see this critic, who despised criticism, and 'never cared for literature as such', walking, always in advance, the main route of the younger generation. He was one of the first to make his exit from the nineteenth century, and to join hands with its more just and quieter predecessor in a mode so quickly fashionable that one has doubts sometimes if it can be right. 'Your creed comes easy to me,' he wrote to Mr. Lytton Strachey, when *Eminent Victorians* appeared, and that symptomatic book had no swifter, more understanding or more appreciative reader. He seemed always, by his own paths, to have reached the next stile, and to be leaning there, as the young wits and adventurers climbed over. It is an attitude in which one may leave him, with great content.

XI

GERARD MANLEY HOPKINS AND ROBERT BRIDGES[1]

MY subject to-day is one which has been long in my mind, but on which you may well discover that I have not attained lucidity, for indeed it has its problems of presentation. I am to speak of the friendship, collaboration, and some of the experimental work for poetry generally of Robert Bridges and Gerard Hopkins —two men who must always have a particular interest for Oxford (which bred them), though their lives and achievement are now the property of the world. The whole matter has been illuminated in the last three or four years by the publication of Hopkins's letters and notebooks, of which the full import has not yet been absorbed. They are not only a piece of literature in themselves, and a contribution to the national history of genius, but as an unstudied picture of Poets at work and in the making they are a school of instruction to all students and practitioners of English verse. The business of *ars poetica* can seldom have been so frankly debated or so starkly laid bare.

Let us say first what first needs saying. It is to the patient and understanding loyalty of Robert Bridges— who was not a patient man—that we owe not only much of Hopkins's work (for Bridges was in effect his audience), but the preservation, also, of most of his poems and letters, the faultless editing of those poems, and the gradual establishment of his fame. This is something to which I shall return; but I emphasize it now because, since Hopkins was, as we say, 'discovered', the part played in this matter by Bridges has been

[1] Lecture from the Chair of Poetry in the University of Oxford, 7 June 1938.

the subject of so many unworthy, misleading, and irresponsible statements—statements in which inaccuracy and ingratitude contend for mastery, and which are only to be excused by slovenly pleas of haste and ignorance.

Bridges and Hopkins first met as freshmen at Oxford, in the year 1863, and might have been expected to drift apart, so different were their routes in life. That indeed very nearly happened. They belonged to a set of able and amusing people who were serious about serious things: about religion and the arts. The Oxford Movement, which in its own peculiar and suffusive way comprehended both these inspirations, had by no means spent its force. Most of these young men composed—with brush or pencil, in music or in verse— and most of them also—even Bridges for a time—like Morris and Burne-Jones a decade earlier, believed themselves destined for Holy Orders: for the cassock of the priest or the habit of a monk. Hopkins's youthful conversion to Romanism, therefore, surprised few of his friends; there were others besides him; but the decision, so characteristic of him, to press the point home, to push the argument to extremity, and, by becoming a Jesuit, take the hardest path—this was felt to be another matter. Intimacy was for a time intimidated; Bridges drew back; and, though they sometimes met, six letters in as many years seem to have been all that then passed between these later voluminous and eager correspondents. This was a barrier which by its nature could never be wholly removed. Bridges, moreover, had sturdy Protestant suspicions, which did not grow less, and which he was ill at concealing. He bitterly grudged a man of genius like Hopkins, an artist of a nature so sensitive and rare, to a system which, while he lived, ignored the meaning (the *divine* meaning) of his gifts, and could only wear him out. And he objected to having his letters opened.

The range of their friendship, though never the force of their affection, was proportionately restricted.

What brought them together again was poetry, and the discovery that, quite unknown to each other, they had been experimenting to some extent in the same things: studying the masterly fingering of Milton's pattern-variations, and the possibility of refreshing, with runlets from the river of speech, the somewhat pampered and jaded rhythms of Victorian verse—of bringing rain, by whatever by-ways, to its roots.

It had been a discovery to Hopkins that Bridges was a poet at all—Bridges, who had been a furtive verse-writer from boyhood. 'I heard of you lately from an Eton and Oxford man I met', Hopkins writes in 1874, 'so and so, he told me, breeds fowls and Bridges writes': and there, to prove it, in the *Academy* of the week before was a review of R. B.'s first book of poems. (Bridges, at Oxford, seems to have admitted only to musical composition—airs and melodies, much prized by Hopkins, and since, I think destroyed).

The hard work of their professions—Bridges in London hospitals and Hopkins in the Jesuit Theological College in Wales—again suspended communication, and it was not till three years later, in 1877, when they were men of 33, that their correspondence took grip and became a working critical alliance. The determining event was once more a book of Bridges, his *Growth of Love*, then in its first slimness. Hopkins was exalted. 'The Sonnets are truly beautiful, breathing a grave and feeling genius, and make me proud of you—which by the by (he adds) is not the same as for you to be proud of yourself: I say it because you always were . . . given to conceit.' [Nothing, you see, like having been undergraduates together!] A 'junk of a letter' followed, 'laden to her gunwales with judicious remarks'. The hunger with which Hopkins leaps at the chance of discussing, with a friend and fellow-craftsman, things so near his heart, and so remote from his vocation and surroundings, is to me very pathetic. The precision and authority of his observations must have revealed to Bridges, if he ever doubted it, a critical intelligence of the first order, and one, moreover, already farther advanced and more perilously occupied on the same tracks of exploration as himself: deep in the Miltonic rhythms, proclaiming, indeed, a knowledge of their last, their parting secret, in the choruses of *Samson Agonistes*, and in firm and determined possession of the principles of a new prosody more audacious and uncompromising than he yet ventured to disclose.

'It happened that the other day, before you had written to me on the matter, I composed two sonnets with rhythmical experiments of the sort, which I think I will presently enclose. How our wits jump! Not but what I have long been on metrical experiments more advanced than these. You will see that my rhythms go further than yours do in the way of irregularity.'

Meanwhile his blessings on Bridges's Muse, and his 'flowing and never-failing music'. Anyone who knew Hopkins will recognize in 'flowing' no common praise. The word was almost technical with him: all nature flows, and so, as in those moving clouds and waters and swaying tree-tops—so, in whatever idiom, should art.

The Sonnets sent must have been, I think, *God's Grandeur* and *The Starlight Night*. Bridges had kept poems of Hopkins's from their undergraduate times, but these were in another world of experience and performance. Let *God's Grandeur* show what he was feeling and doing in this new world.

> The world is charged with the grandeur of God.
>   It will flame out, like shining from shook foil;
>   It gathers to a greatness, like the ooze of oil
> Crushed. Why do men then now not reck his rod?

Generations have trod, have trod, have trod;
   And all is seared with trade; bleared, smeared with toil;
   And wears man's smudge and shares man's smell: the soil
Is bare now, nor can foot feel, being shod.

And for all this, nature is never spent;
   There lives the dearest freshness deep down things;
And though the last lights off the black West went
   Oh, morning, at the brown brink eastward, springs—
Because the Holy Ghost over the bent
   World broods with warm breast and with ah! bright wings.

This fine poem, written freely from the heart, without
strain or contortion, is described by Hopkins as in
'Standard Rhythm counterpointed', i.e. with those
reversions of accent which give two concurrent scan-
sions, a heard and an unheard.   In other words, it is
technically an application of the Miltonic discovery of
which I spoke, a discovery recorded with honour in
Bridges's treatise on *Milton's Prosody*.   The choruses in
Samson Agonistes, so long complained of for capricious
irregularity, Hopkins perceived to have a system.   Milton, in these freer lyric parts, was experimenting with
variations of natural English stress rhythms.   The
iambic measure, where it seems to disappear, is in fact
preserved as a fictitious structure, never heard but only
counted, 'a scansion not intended to be read, but to be
imagined as a time-beat on which the free rhythm is
syncopated, as a melody'.

We are familiar now with this notion of counter-
pointing which Milton practised, though with more
restraint, in his epics also, so familiar indeed that
Hopkins's sonnet would never be remarked on to-day
as an experiment.   But these things were once news!
When the first version of Bridges's later treatise appeared in 1887, some young poets, he tells us, counterpointed so much, took to using Miltonic inversions so
freely, that champions of the prevailing orthodoxy
raised an indignant protest in the Press, and the dis-

cussion grew so hot that a London evening journal actually advertised Prosody as a feature in its daily posters.

If it be true what my colleague Mr. Lewis asserts, and he has great experience, that the modern undergraduate is entirely ignorant of Prosody, I see no sign of such things happening again. I am sorry if it is so; for though Prosody in cold blood is a trying business, and Rhythm is so much more 'evident', and 'seems to lie so much nearer to the poetic effects', yet Rhythm is not verse, and cannot possibly become so until ordered by Prosody. I suppose this neglect of structure, of anatomy, of the grammar of verse, is part of what is called the classical decline; but it cannot be unconnected with our growing habituation to the boneless wonders of modern verse. Most modern poets speak only of rhythms and textures—whatever those are—and many in their practice seem almost to stop there. A story is told of Isaac Vossius, the Dutch scholar, that he had his hair combed by the rules of prosody, having lighted on certain barbers and bathmen who could, in combing, 'imitate iambics, trochèes and dactyls: from whence (he assures us) there arose to me no small delight'. For the deplorable situation described by Mr. Lewis this suggests, at least provisionally, a remedy, a way out.

The two sonnets sent to Bridges seemed to Hopkins, no doubt, more appropriate first messengers than the advanced experiments to which he had so darkly alluded. Of these he still withheld, though he had finished it a year before, the capital example—what was to remain, in fact, of all his applications of what he already called 'the new Prosody', the longest and most fully orchestrated—I mean *The Wreck of the Deutschland*. At last it was sent off, and ten months later they were still disputing about it. Bridges's first response to this packed, tremendous, almost terrifying and sometimes repellent composition was a parody, and a refusal to read it twice. 'Your parody reassures me', said Hopkins, 'about your understanding the metre.' He rejects the forgivable charge that, judged by this poem, there was no conceivable licence that he might not justify. 'I am stricter than you and I might say than anybody I know.' Read it again, he pleads, and not merely with the eyes. It is less to be read than heard; its rhythm is oratorical. If it is obscure, don't bother for the moment with the meaning. So far as that is accessible—and it isn't always, and wasn't meant to be—it will come. At any rate he will alter nothing. Why should he? 'I do not write for the public. You are my public, and I hope to convert you.'

To the new system of prosody in which this and many of his later poems were written, Hopkins, as you know, gave the name of *Sprung Rhythm*—meaning by 'sprung', he says, something like 'abrupt'. His own accounts of it may be found in his published letters, and more formally and accessibly in the document which Bridges extracted from him and which appears as 'Author's Preface' in the edition of his poems. I cannot now go fully into this, but briefly it consists in scanning by accents or stresses alone, without account of the number of syllables as in common rhythm, so that a foot may be one strong syllable, or it may be one strong and many light. He did not claim, of course, to have invented *sprung rhythms* but only *sprung rhythm*, single lines of it being common enough in nursery rhymes and popular jingles, and in the poets themselves. 'One, two, Buckle my shoe'—this has it. Or from Campbell, 'And their fleet along the deep proudly shone'. Or from Shakespeare, 'Why should this desert be?' But no one had professedly used it and made it a principle throughout. In the *Deutschland* and other pieces he claimed to have enfranchised these stragglers, and made them a regular and permanent principle of scansion.

To the question, why employ Sprung Rhythm at all, his answer was that it is the nearest to the native and natural rhythm of speech, the least forced, the most rhetorical and emphatic of all possible rhythms.

How then had the Poets missed it? If they could have done it, he says, they would. Many people were, as the phrase is, 'burning', took it up and mislaid it.

Had it any history: anything that could be called a literary ancestry? Yes! Greek and Latin lyric were clearly in sprung rhythm; so was old English verse as seen surviving in *Piers Plowman*; but it had ceased to be used since the Elizabethan Age, Greene being the last writer who could be said to have recognized it.

A strange story which I am afraid I don't believe! But it would take too long to go into that. Let us listen to the rhythm.

The Wreck of The Deutschland

(1) Part I   1
(Invocation)
> Thou mastering me
> God! giver of breath and bread;
> World's strand, sway of the sea;
> Lord of living and dead;
> Thou hast bound bones and veins in me, fastened me flesh,
> And after it almost unmade, what with dread,
> Thy doing: and dost thou touch me afresh?
> Over again I feel thy finger and find thee.

2
> I did say yes
> O at lightning and lashed rod;
> Thou heardst me truer than tongue confess
> Thy terror, O Christ, O God;
> Thou knowest the walls, altar and hour and night:
> The swoon of a heart that the sweep and the hurl of thee trod
> Hard down with a horror of height:
> And the midriff astrain with leaning of, laced with fire of stress.

3

The frown of his face
Before me, the hurtle of hell
Behind, where, where was a, where was a place?
I whirled out wings that spell
And fled with a fling of the heart to the heart of the Host.
My heart, but you were dovewinged, I can tell,
Carrier-witted, I am bold to boast,
To flash from the flame to the flame then, tower from the grace
to the grace.

5

I kiss my hand
To the stars, lovely-asunder
Starlight, wafting him out of it; and
Glow, glory in thunder;
Kiss my hand to the dappled-with-damson west:
Since, tho' he is under the world's splendour and wonder,
His mystery must be instressed, stressed;
For I greet him the days I meet him, and bless when I under-
stand.

9

Be adored among men,
God, three-numberèd form;
Wring thy rebel, dogged in den,
Man's malice, with wrecking and storm.
Beyond saying sweet, past telling of tongue,
Thou art lightning and love, I found it, a winter and warm;
Father and fondler of heart thou hast wrung:
Hast thy dark descending and most art merciful then.

Part II
(Refrain)

11

'Some find me a sword; some
The flange and the rail; flame,
Fang or flood' goes Death on drum,
And storms bugle his fame.
But wé dream we are rooted in earth—Dust!

Flesh falls within sight of us, we, though our flower the same,
  Wave with the meadow, forget that there must
The sour scythe cringe, and the blear share come.

16

    One stirred from the rigging to save
      The wild woman-kind below,
  With a rope's end round the man, handy and brave—
      He was pitched to his death at a blow,
For all his dreadnought breast and braids of thew:
  They could tell him for hours, dandled the to and fro
    Through the cobbled foam-fleece, what could he do
With the burl of the fountains of air, buck and the flood of the
    wave?

(2) Easier:

Pied Beauty

Glory be to God for dappled things—
  For skies of couple-colour as a brinded cow;
    For rose-moles all in stipple upon trout that swim;
Fresh-firecoal chesnut-falls; finches' wings;
  Landscape plotted and pieced—fold, fallow, and plough;
    And áll trádes, their gear and tackle and trim.

All things counter, original, spare, strange;
  Whatever is fickle, freckled (who knows how?)
    With swift, slow; sweet, sour; adazzle, dim;
He fathers-forth whose beauty is past change:
        Praise him.

The Windhover

I caught this morning morning's minion, kingdom of day-
  light's dauphin, dapple-dawn-drawn Falcon in his riding
Of the rolling level underneath him steady air, and striding
High there, how he rung upon the rein of a wimpling wing
In his ecstasy! then off, off forth on swing,
  As a skate's heel sweeps smooth on a bow-bend: the hurl and
    gliding
  Rebuffed the big wind. My heart in hiding
Stirred for a bird,—the achieve of, the mastery of the thing!

As one reads these verses it becomes plain how profoundly they are conditioned, even as metrical compositions, by other things than the new prosody: by a diction now rich, now spare, but always tense, individual, and inventive; by a peculiar way of seeing things, an abnormal vision of the movements and colours of the physical world, and especially of the living creatures in it, and a painter's passion to 'hold' them, to seize them just as they are at that very instant of time, unposed, not studio-muffled, in action, themselves: to the glory of God, no doubt, since all things are created for His glory, but at any rate themselves, flashed there and caught. There is detectable also a devouring and yet noble greed for beauty—of every kind and all at once—which affects even his prosody. His lines must be packed with every metrical attraction: must thud with alliteration, must have every kind of rhyme, end-rhymes, and mid-rhymes, with the fainter luxury of assonance, and even a consonantal chime picked up from Welsh verse. The stanzas or set pieces, moreover, must run, if possible, as scansion without break to the end. There will be rests, also, when required, as in music, and outriding feet (we have heard them in *The Windhover*), slack syllables, light horsemen auxiliaries, not counted in the scansion, which can swing forward or backward as wanted, being conceived as in another dimension than the line itself. And, to conclude, since every ingredient of this ultimate music should have its due, marks of metrical notation should be provided (if only they were less unsightly!) for the trained performer who is to recite the poem. He does not expect us to be able to read his poems as reading is commonly understood. They are works for performance and should have *opus* numbers. You must first discover what their rhythm and tempi are, then learn how to deliver each sentence with the rhythm and tempo it requires. Moreover, to

understand the rhythm of the words you must understand their meaning, though that in turn is partly
derived from the rhythm. These requirements, which
are too much, I fear, for me, are not novel in principle:
any fine piece of verse deserves, at any rate, that *kind*
of care. The novelty is in the pressure put on them,
and the degree of technical virtuosity Hopkins asks for.

Bridges recovered from the first shock of the *Deutschland*, and on further acquaintance recognized its pri-
mary importance in the history of Hopkins's art,

'The labour spent on this great metrical experiment', he
wrote, 'must have served to establish the poet's prosody and
perhaps his diction: therefore the poem stands logically as
well as chronologically in the front of his book, like a great
dragon folded in the gate to forbid all entrance, and confident
in its strength from past success.'

He advises readers to circumvent him and attack him
later in the rear. It is what he did himself. Presently
he was experimenting on his own account in Sprung
Rhythm, with notable but less shattering effect: taking
just as much of the system as he could use, within the
classic delicacy of his own style. His debt to Hopkins
he publicly acknowledged and deplored that such originals should be still in manuscript. Hopkins's reception
of these attempts in what he calls 'mitigated Sprung
Rhythm' was as warm as could be expected of such a
die-hard inventor. Bridges treated it in theory and
practice as something informal and variable without
any limit but ear and taste: but Hopkins stood out for
the fantastic rigour of his law. He praised, however,
such pieces as *London Snow*, which with some others of
its kind, just because it was mitigated, did more than
anything else to insinuate into poetic practice in the
eighties and nineties the new music of speech-rhythms.

So they went on, with alternate encouragement and
laceration, as friends should: Bridges more and more
aware that he had to do with potentially the finest

poet of his day, and Hopkins happily applausive of a style so different from his own, so pure and yet so flowing. 'What fun', he cries, when *Prometheus* came out—'what fun if you should be a classic!' They formed a little circle as time went on with Canon Dixon and, later, Patmore, and it is amusing to see how promptly Gerard Hopkins became the retained and masterly critic of them all. They pressed him to publish, and Bridges, by some ingenuity, to pave the way for his reception, entangled him in correspondence with some of the leading reviewers of the day. But it was useless. He pleaded with growing despondency his incompatible vocation—sent his pieces to Bridges without even caring to keep a copy—and did his best to pretend that he was content with that audience, since 'a poet is a public in himself'. The last years of his life were darkened by growing weakness and despair and in 1889 he died, in Ireland. Some sonnets were found among his papers which record the deadly misery of that time. They are hard to read even now, carry out no prosodic theory, and are among the finest of his poems.

It must always be regretted that Bridges, who abhorred the thought of becoming the subject of a biography, should for that reason have destroyed his letters to Hopkins, which were returned to him after Hopkins's death. It was clearly from no critical vanity that he acted as he did, for all the pungencies of Hopkins are preserved intact. It was give and take between them. If Bridges made fun of the *Deutschland* Hopkins had his turn when Bridges's *Prometheus* came along.

'From high Olympus and the domeless courts' it began.

'*Domeless.*' Wrote Hopkins. 'If there were some reason for it why do you not tell me? A court I suppose to be any large room or space of a building upon the ground floor and imperfectly closed. About the being on the ground floor I do not feel quite sure, about the being imperfectly closed—above or around —I do. Courts can seldom be domed in any case, so that it is needless to tell us that those on Olympus are domeless. No: better to say the kamptuliconless courts or Minton's-encaustic-tileless courts or vulcanised-india-rubberless courts. This would strike a keynote at once and bespeak attention. And if the critics said those things did not belong to the period you would have (as you have now with *domeless*) the overwhelming answer, that you never said they did but the contrary, and that Prometheus, who was at once a prophet and as a mechanician more than equal to Edison and the Jablochkoff candle and the Moc-main Patent Lever Truss with self-adjusting duplex gear and attachments, meant to say that emphatically they had *not* got those improvements on Olympus and he did not intend that they should. But if you cannot see your way to this "frank" treatment and are inclined to think that fault might be found with *domeless*, then remember that the fault is found *in your first line.*'

It was changed to 'ætherial'.

Hopkins was not much in sympathy with the Grecian mythology, and on occasion made Bridges pay for it. As on *Eros and Psyche*. 'Eros is little more than a winged Masher, but Psyche is a success, a sweet little "body", rather than "soul".' I have no doubt that he paid for that in Bridges's next letter.

Though he had admired *Prometheus the Firegiver* he would not pretend to like *Ulysses*.

'Believe me, the Greek gods are a totally unworkable material: the merest frigidity, which must chill and kill every living work of art they are brought into. Even if we put aside the hideous and, taken as they stand, unspeakable stories told of them, which stories nevertheless are as authentic as their names and person-alities—both are equally imaginary; if you do not like that, both equally symbolical—, putting them out of sight and look-ing only at their respectable side, they are poor ignoble concep-tions ennobled bodily only (as if they had bodies) by the artists, but once in motion and action worthless—not gentlemen or ladies, cowards, loungers, without majesty, without awe, antiquity, foresight, character; old bucks, young bucks and Biddy Buckskins. What did Athene do after leaving Ulysses? Lounged back to Olympus to afternoon nectar. Nothing can be made of it. May 21, 1885. The background of distance and darkness and doom which a tragedy should always have is shut out by an Olympian drop-scene; the characters from men become puppets, their bloodshed becomes a leakage of bran. (This, upon my word, is to ply the lash and be unpardonable.) I see the nobility of the rest, but this one touch to my eye spoils all.'

It is the same writer who signs himself 'Kindly also be damned to you for not writing and believe me affectionately yours' and who was asked by Bridges four months later to be his Best Man. I know nothing of these things, but it must be an uncommon request to make to a Jesuit Father. The year was 1884.

Nothing is more notable in Robert Bridges's long life than his care for his friends while living and for their memory when dead. It was he more than any other, once Hopkins had made them acquainted, who made Dixon known—though I am afraid, to a very small public. His memoirs and editions of Dixon, and of his school friend Dolben, are classics of criticism and friendship. Of Hopkins unfortunately he wrote no similar account, but that he intended to do so there is no doubt. I think this has never been stated, but I have seen the letters addressed to Provost Daniel of Worcester—proposing, as early as 20 August 1889, within a month or two of Hopkins's death, that he should print at his press a memoir of Hopkins, with a selection from his poems. 'It will be a unique volume', he wrote. On 11 October he reports that he can send the poems any day, and the memoir possibly by January. Why this project fell through I have no knowledge: at any rate some hindrance occurred, and Bridges had to take other and more gradual ways of making known to a public unacquainted even with his name the most revolutionary poet of his day, and, at first sight, by far the most uncouth. It could only be done by a kind of honest stealth. In 1890 he dedicated to his memory a book of his own poems, and in 1894 secured admission for eleven of his pieces, and for a biographical notice which he supplied, in Miles's *Poets and Poetry of the Nineteenth Century*. So the work went on. In 1894, finding that his friend Beeching was making two anthologies, he saw that something from Hopkins went into each. 'We shall see how Hopkins is received', he wrote. 'It might be that there was a call for more.' Interest slowly grew; his co-religionaries took him up; and curiosity was confirmed by his inclusion in 1915, in the Poet Laureate's *Spirit of Man*. Three years later appeared Bridges's edition of his *Poems*. 'It was undertaken', he says, 'in response to a demand that, both in England and in America, has gradually grown up from the genuinely poetic interest felt in the poems which I have gradually introduced to the public.' This masterly edition was made from autographic manuscripts in his possession, most of which would have been lost but for his care.

Bridges has been so often reproached for not producing this edition earlier that it is of interest to know how it sold. I take my figures from Professor Abbott's admirable edition of the letters. Seven hundred and fifty copies were printed, of which 50 were given away. There sold, in the first year, 180; in the second, 240; then an average for six years of 30 a year, rising to 90 in 1927. The last 4 copies sold in 1928. This does not suggest any *hunger* in the nation to read Hopkins. The sale, in fact, is what might have been expected, though one critic, Mr. Middleton Murry, writing in 1919, gave it as his opinion that if Hopkins had not had 'Mr. Bridges, who was his friend, to stand sponsor, and the Oxford University Press to stand the racket' (that is the phrase), he would still have been condemned to obscurity.

The 'discovery' of Hopkins by the young lies within the last ten years. His day had come, and he has burst on them in the right way. I would ask you to observe how beautifully it has all been timed, and by how wise and Fabian a general! There is even more to it than that. If these indignant young gentlemen, who must always have a grievance, had ears to hear the novel music of Hopkins they have to thank for that, more than any other man, his friend, Robert Bridges.

XII

JOHN SWINNERTON PHILLIMORE[1]

ELEVEN years ago my predecessor of that time in the Chair of Poetry, Mr. Garrod of Merton, in one of his admirable lectures, stepped aside for a moment to look at the vexed and sometimes derided question of the academic poet. The date was December 1926, when the untimely death of the distinguished scholar and poet on whom I desire to address you was still freshly and cruelly present to all who had known him here. The lecturer had been speaking, in the same breath, of the poetry of the war period, then only eight years distant, and of colleges as habitations for poets. Though far from suggesting that a college or, I suppose, academic society generally is, upon the whole, the best place for a poet, he was, as I understood him, no less unwilling to accept the vulgar belief that such poetic habitation spells either failure or frigidity. He had, indeed, as he explained, vivid and recent evidence to the contrary. It so happens, he said, 'that the three poets of whom I think most often in connexion with the war, and with the least reserve in my appreciation, are three Fellows of Colleges'. One was Mr. Housman, another was Mr. Phillimore, and the third was Rupert Brooke.

'Perhaps no short occasional poem', he continued, 'was ever so direct in its effectiveness as the *Epitaph on a Mercenary Army*. Very different in character, of larger compass, more intricately laboured—indeed, too curious in its craftsmanship—but yet a great poem, was Mr. Phillimore's poem upon the death of Charles Fisher. When it first appeared, a critic . . . spoke of it in *The Times* as the noblest poem which the war had produced.

[1] Lecture from the Chair of Poetry in the University of Oxford, November 1937, revised.

The poem is still not so well known as it should be; and the same is true of other poems of Mr. Phillimore. It is a fault of the time—not enough people take trouble to distinguish, in poetry, good from bad. Mr. Phillimore's death, three weeks ago, was a very real loss to English letters; and a very real loss to Oxford. ἀγαθὸς ποιητὴς καὶ ποθεινὸς τοῖς φίλοις. Though he had been gone from Oxford five and twenty years, many of us here knew him well—the man, and the poetry that was in him. Perhaps he was not easy to know well; just as his poetry is not, I think, easy to read. Both as a man and as a literary artist he was reserved. His character and his craftsmanship alike (he was essentially a craftsman) had a quality of reserve akin to the antique. But both invited and rewarded affectionate study. At least the poem I have mentioned will not easily be let die.'

I have cited this tribute at length because it is quiet and measured, and gives an honest starting-point; because, though so closely contemporary with its subject's death, it has none of the weaknesses which haunt obituary judgements; because it is the tribute of perhaps the best qualified of his friends, as fellow-scholar and poet, as English critic and Latinist, to estimate the range and efficacy of Mr. Phillimore's gifts. I could wish for that reason that he were your lecturer to-day. But I should still be discontented, for I owe a debt to Mr. Phillimore which can only be paid, if at all, in person, and in some such manner as this. It has been long in my mind, and still longer on my conscience, to present, if I could, and present publicly, in his old University—in the University which his family have frequented and adorned for six generations—some picture of a man who in his youth represented the very flower and finer spirit of the old Oxford, and in his overtasked maturity, in the intervals of commanding, as none before had ever commanded, one of the most turbulent democracies in the world—I mean, the Humanity or Latin class-room of the University of Glasgow—maintained in his adopted country of Scotland, in season and out, and often beyond his strength, the faith that was in him and the cause of humanism everywhere. Of this ripe devotion and expense of spirit, though its fruits yet live, we have only fragments in print: occasional and still scattered papers and prefaces—pungent, challenging, brimming with ideas—in which he distilled his scholarship, and, for his more private satisfaction, poems which, though partially collected, are even less known to-day than when Mr. Garrod spoke. I am not without hope that this attempt of mine, however modest and provisional, to direct attention to Mr. Phillimore's writing generally, may advance the day of a Select Collection of his prose and verse.

Of one embarrassment I am very conscious. There are in this audience some who by right of family, or of faith, or through advantages of seniority, knew him as I never could. There are others, once his students like myself, but the more brilliant harvest of his prime, now administering learning in various colleges in Oxford, who could tell me much, no doubt, that did not fall within my experience. To all these, should I be so unhappy as to offer them nothing new, I would plead the propriety of addressing myself first to that portion of my audience to whom Mr. Phillimore's name and work are possibly as yet unknown. And here let me announce the opportune appearance, in the new volume, just issued, of the *Dictionary of National Biography*, of a life of Mr. Phillimore, brief, as that scheme demands, but clearly and sensitively drawn. Though this cannot absolve me from some of the duties of a biographer, I am glad to be able to refer you to it.

'I believe,' said Mr. Phillimore, addressing, on the 25th of January 1905, a delighted gathering of the Govan Burns Club, 'I believe that in all the poetry of Burns there is only one English dwelling house mentioned by name: that is the house where I was born in

Cornwall.' He would not insult (he added) a company
of professed initiates by reminding them of the place
or of the passage. The place is Boconnoc, a residence
of his Fortescue relatives. He was born in 1873, of a
family which had long been distinguished for public
service in Church and State, in the Navy and Army, at
the Bar and on the Bench, and in the pursuit of letters,
and there was a time in early manhood, and even beyond, when he was troubled by this rich variety of
inherited aptitudes and examples. How determine between their conflicting appeals? But I am forgetting
the schoolboy. 'Not to name the school or the masters
of men illustrious for literature,' says Dr. Johnson, 'is a
kind of historical fraud, by which honest fame is injuri-
ously diminished.' John Phillimore went to Westminster School, as a Phillimore must, and was an early
and favourite pupil of that remarkable scholar and
headmaster, Dr. W. G. Rutherford. From Westminster to Christ Church was, again for a Phillimore, an
almost fated transition. He concluded a brilliant
undergraduate career as Ireland, Craven, and Hertford
Scholar, and as President of the Union in one of the
loftiest eras of that oddly undulating institution.
These junior and unruffled triumphs were diversified by
many interesting and some lasting friendships, and not
least by the burlesque harmonies of the Republican
Club. This is that Club of the 'intrepid four' to which,
and to the dissolving fortunes of its members, Mr.
Hilaire Belloc was to dedicate his first volume of verse.

> Not even this peculiar town
> Has ever fixed a friendship firmer,
> But—one is married, one's gone down,
> And one's a Don, and one's in Burmah.

Mr. Belloc's terser epitaph, beginning

> Rub-a-dub-dub,
> The Republican Club,

has not, I think, been printed, and was as impromptu as
it sounds.

The Don was Mr. Phillimore. He became first a
Lecturer and then a Student of Christ Church, and
three years later, in 1899, at the age of 26, went north
to take up the brilliant succession of the Glasgow
Chair of Greek. Though the high compliment of the
appointment was understood—his immediate predecessors had been Gilbert Murray and Richard Jebb—
it is clear that none of his friends for a moment imagined that Glasgow was to keep him and be the scene
of his life. One, evidently suggesting consolations,
wrote: 'I hope you are a fisherman. A Scotch professor
has only to ask to have the best fishing in Scotland.'
Another emphasized the amplitude of the old Scottish
vacations, and urged him to 'let Pluto have his legal
six months, and no more'. All regarded it as an honourable but purely temporary exile, as a wild but
well-paid prelude to a Chair at Oxford and a seat at
Westminster. How English this all is! But then Mr.
Phillimore, though very soon he could not be torn
from Glasgow, was very English too. That debate, for
example, between the active and the contemplative
life, between scholarship and politics, how much more
it has tormented Englishmen than any other race! It
may be heard, while he was still an undergraduate, in
the best of his early poems, *In a Meadow*, the only piece
of his, I think, to enter the standard anthologies.
Fortunately Sir Arthur Quiller-Couch has always read
his *Oxford Magazine*, and by that route the poem
reached his *Oxford Book of Victorian Verse*.

> This is the place
> Where far from the unholy populace
> The daughter of Philosophy and Sleep
>   Her court doth keep,
> Sweet Contemplation. To her service bound
>   Hover around

The little amiable summer airs,
        Her courtiers.

The deep black soil
Makes mute her palace-floors with thick trefoil;
The grasses sagely nodding overhead
        Curtain her bed;
And lest the feet of strangers overpass
        Her walls of grass,
Gravely a little river goes his rounds
        To beat the bounds.

—No bustling flood
To make a tumult in her neighbourhood,
But such a stream as knows to go and come
        Discreetly dumb.
Therein are chambers tapestried with weeds
        And screened with reeds;
For roof the waterlily-leaves serene
        Spread tiles of green.

The sun's large eye
Falls soberly upon me where I lie;
For delicate webs of immaterial haze
        Refine his rays.
The air is full of music none knows what,
        Or half-forgot;
The living echo of dead voices fills
        The unseen hills.

I hear the song
Of cuckoo answering cuckoo all day long;
And know not if it be my inward sprite
        For my delight
Making remembered poetry appear
        As sound in the ear:
Like a salt savour poignant in the breeze
        From distant seas.

Dreams without sleep,
And sleep too clear for dreaming and too deep;
And Quiet very large and manifold
        About me rolled;

Satiety, that momentary flower,
   Stretched to an hour:
These are her gifts which all mankind may use,
   And all refuse.

This finely tempered and delicately modulated poem was written in 1894, and, when one has allowed for reminiscence, is still a remarkable production for a young man of 21.

He seemed at that time, and for the next five years, to have the world for his choice, though 'the stillness of divine studies' had already, I think, as good as claimed him. Yet the five years were all experiment. He travelled over Italy, collating manuscripts of Propertius and Statius especially, both of whom he was to edit, and, as his diary notes, 'saw the great Mommsen, aureoled in a fringe of long white hair, working diligently his four morning hours at the Vatican'. Politics intervening, he contributed with Mr. Belloc, Mr. John Simon and others, to a volume of Liberal Essays, writing on British Foreign Policy, and on the heels of this, in collaboration with his old tutor and colleague, Mr. S. G. Owen of Christ Church, produced *Musa Clauda*, one of the most elegant of all the Oxford collections of Latin elegiac verse. The excitement and appeasement of metrical composition was always a necessity to him, and most of the pieces in his first book of English poems, the volume of 1902, were written at this time in Italy or Oxford. He belonged to the newly founded Horace Club, of which the only properties were an urn and a book, and where members chosen by lot read aloud their verses. The charge of obscurity, which he was so often to incur, was already familiar; it came indeed from all quarters. 'Mr. Phillimore', says the *Isis* (he was one of the Idols of 1895), 'has written verses in the manner of himself.' A Balliol friend announces, writing from Vincent's of all places: 'A Phillimore Club has been started to study your poems.' 'Belloc arrived', says a diary of 1898, 'and damned some of my verses for obscurity.' Meanwhile he taught and lectured, adding Russian, at odd times, to his already impressive complement of languages. And when friends, books, pupils, politics became suddenly too much for him, he escaped to the pure sensation of the Alps, to

'the tense delight of desperate finger-tips,
The lithe advance, and just finesse of poise.'

There he was in his glory. Craftsmanship, in which he never failed, whether he were writing a poem or whittling a stick, soon placed him among the most accomplished and original climbers of his time. He was consulted by the great Coolidge himself; and in his favourite Dolomites a *via Phillimore* still commemorates one of his choicest and most admired ascents.

Glasgow, I am afraid, arrested most of these diversions. He had stooped to the load; and I doubt if he ever seriously climbed again. His promised book on the Dolomites was abandoned. And after some years of prominence in West of Scotland politics he lost interest in party also.

I was a member of his first class at the University of Glasgow (we met at eight in the morning), and vividly recall what seemed the miracle of his apparition. So this, we said, with excitement and a sigh of pleasure, is that fabled and desirable thing, the perfect Oxford man! From every feature, tone and movement, in their finished perfection and repose, it was plain to the most jealous (and we were sturdy defenders of our own less mellowed civilization) that this was something beyond our range, that here England had done her best and had succeeded. It was an interesting moment in the history of the University. There was a change of fashion and of dynasty in the literary theatres of the Faculty of which even we freshmen were aware.

A. C. Bradley and Gilbert Murray retired, and Walter Raleigh and J. S. Phillimore came in. I need not dwell on the good fortune of the place in having four such men in two successions; what struck us more was the pungency of the change. Truth in both classrooms rested a little from her ecstasies, and became companionable; and Literature was revealed, not primarily as the utterance of a few exalted or distracted moments, but as the great and perpetual mistress of the Art of Living.

The new Professor's Inaugural Lecture on Greek Studies was long remembered, and one sentence at least is still quoted in Oxford. 'I had rather', he said, 'a young man knew a single book of Homer than that he should dig up and date all the crockery in the Archipelago; familiarly enjoy Pericles' Funeral Oration, or any of the well-worn, well-proved treasures of literature, than scratch at all the conjectural sites of all the battles in the Peloponnesian War.' Archaeology, what Verrall called 'stuffage', was then the new idol of the classical world, and seemed to this lecturer to have forgotten its place. His subject was Hellenism, and not the Hellenism of Pater, but 'a perfection, a finish, put on Nature's force and health'. Idiom was the life of it. It embraced Aristophanes as congenially as Plato, and was more clearly to be seen 'in *A Shropshire Lad* than in *Atalanta in Calydon*, in the prose of Newman and Stevenson than in *Marius the Epicurean*'. We thought, I remember, as we listened to him, that this would do.

Into the history of his twenty-seven years at Glasgow I can enter only lightly. With the young men he was nobly successful from the first. The raw student who came, according to northern tradition, to riot and barbarize, was startled to find that he was making, instead, his first acquaintance with civilization, and liking it. In 1906, on the retirement of Professor Ramsay, he had transferred from the Greek to the Latin Classroom. It was the right choice, for the core of his studies had always been Latinity—the Latin tongue and the Roman temper. Daily, session by session, we are told, his students greeted him with stirring song, and, when he so willed it, were on the instant hushed to attention. When he said 'Gentlemen' in a certain way, the effect was that of Caesar's *Quirites*. Holding, as he did, that the young lions and eagles must be fed on freshly killed meat, he was fastidious even to a fault in his preparation of their diet. His lectures were enriched by private reading which broke everywhere through the 'sacred pales', the artificial enclosures of the classical 'Golden Ages', and ranged the whole field of the ancient and early Christian world. He was never in the habit of asking too narrowly of what metal his Latin might be. Those old deterrents, 'Silver' and 'Brazen', weighed little with a student who was *domesticus Fidei*, who read Latin not only as the literary language of Rome, but as the mother tongue of Christendom, and was as familiar, one felt, with Prudentius as with Catullus, with St. Augustine as with Cicero, and on as intimate terms with Petrarch and the humanists as with the models whom they followed. It was a reproach often on his lips that men should pass for good classics to whom Latin was a closed book after Hadrian, and Prudentius (let us say) a dangerous person because, not content with the unclassical awkwardness of being a Christian, he scans *idola* as a dactyl, which was how, in fact, it was then pronounced.

The fine and catholic curiosity which he brought to these studies guided him also to the niceties of the modern tongues. In English he was, both orally and in writing, a finished master. His subtle craftsmanship in English verse, which will one day be better recognized, has been obscured by perversities of experiment and by the difficulty of some of his effects. But indeed he courted difficulty. He was perfectly acquainted

with the French and Italian languages, and enjoyed
using them and translating from them, though he
confessed that an oversensitiveness to idiom and to the
shyer associations of words (which haunted him also in
Latin) tended sometimes to embarrass his renderings.
'I think', he said, 'that I translate best from Russian,
because I don't know it too well.' Most of us weigh
words as we weigh parcels, content with rough ap-
proximations. He was delicate in these matters even
to excess, but for that reason he made scholars, and
may yet instruct poets.

His first volume of poems appeared in 1902, and was
dedicated to Mr. Belloc. There are scholars who keep
their learning and their poetry apart. Mr. Housman
keeps the two almost savagely distinct: there is his
'pedantry', as he calls it, and, at long intervals, his
poetry. In Phillimore, the one played always with the
other; indeed, whatever he might be doing, poetry was
sure to slip in. Drafts of English verses may be found
in his earliest diaries alongside reports of mountain
routes and weather. They lurk in his most erudite
note-books, entangled with memoranda on some usage
of St. Augustine or Arnobius. In this first volume of
verse it would, I think, be uncritical to suggest that,
besides the poem *In A Meadow*, there is much more to
be found than the evidence of keen senses, of a young
man's *malaise*, and of high technical accomplishment.
One piece only I will cite because I have always liked
and remembered it:

A Bicycle Ride on the Appia Nuova

Eventide puts all the mills to sleep,
When quietly the harass'd waters creep
To comb their crystal tresses at the weirs.
All day an outlaw, Peace at eve appears:
No drudge mechanic but at evening shelves
His trade—the hour when men may be themselves—
And handles happiness awhile.

And I
Italian hearted with Italian sky,
At evening felt the cranks and wheels of Reason
Muffle their angry travail for a season;
And, all the scolding tongues of Reason mute,
Tasted pleasure and knowledge absolute.
Each brutish pore grown wiser than the mind,
Pure single spirit the league of sense combined.
    The leaves of spring were tender as the beams
Of sunlight on the floor of shallow streams;
On blossomed almond orchards changed the flush;
Sweet from the bean-fields came the throb and rush
In my ear and over my cheek of the breeze
Stroking the plain with breath of placid seas.
Red with the sunset still beside the road
Rome in innumerable arches strode;
Each white acclivity of town that fills
The shadowy creases in the Alban hills,
Six leagues away seemed just a stone's-throw distant.
    Master of life and free of all existent,
Thanking God for awhile to know and feel,
Silent I slid upon my twinkling wheel.

The author of the recent Life in the *Dictionary of National Biography* remarks a change of mind in his poetry after a certain year, and very properly connects that change with the most important event in his spiritual history. In 1905 he was received into the Roman Church. It was a decision which, I believe, surprised none of his intimates; it gave him great peace of mind, and, what he craved, a living cause to serve. In this cause he welcomed the humblest as well as the highest duties, and when he died there was no layman in the Roman Catholic community of Scotland more honoured, more influential, or more loved. His latest verse, not yet collected, is deeply coloured by his faith, and may well be found to contain some of his strongest work.

I have rewarded myself lately by choosing some

characteristic sentences from his scattered essays and papers: as thus on the white-washers of Robert Burns:

'It seems foolish and graceless to apologize for a conflagration when a century of posterity has warmed both hands with joy before it.'

Or on the seamy side of academic Research:

'We have lived to see dulness, under polite aliases, dignified almost as a religion; bright young intelligences labouring to be dull, and will not be comforted because they are not.'

On the true meaning of 'Attic':

'Attic is the most Greek of Greek . . . and its essence is that Art or Science (which in a Romantic view are enemies) here are sisters: beauty and truth—two names for an ideal: writing, just talking immortalized, having shed the triviality and kept the ease.'

On Tradition:

'Tradition is to Art and Letters what Capital is to Economic Man.'

On the life of Verse and Prose:

'As a rule maturity lasts longer in prose than in verse. For prose is an institution. After Lucan nothing of prime greatness is produced in poetry until Prudentius. In Latin Prose, on the other hand, it is simply true to say that St. Jerome and St. Augustine could drive their ships under all the sail that ever Cicero carried.'

On the barriers of Time and Language:

'We have not intimate aesthetic appreciation enough of prose style to taste now in a Dio Chrysostom or an Aelius Aristides what a modern Englishman can still admire in Ruskin. What modern scholar can pretend that the supreme music of Ζέφυροι δ᾽ ἐρήμην καταπνέουσιν does not elude him? And will the Japanese critic of a thousand years hence find anything in Ruskin but the melodious flatulence?'

On translation and the genial larcenies of great poets:

'Perhaps the only perfect translations are the scraps which

poets bring in without acknowledgement: things got in a lusty stealth.

"The world's great age begins anew,
    the golden years return."

Nothing so perfect was ever seen in a professed translation; yet Shelley does not trouble to name Virgil. . . . No acknowledgement is necessary. This is Spartan thieving.'

One other passage. It is on Words and the Forms of Literature, and sums up as well as anything his own artistic theory and creed:

'A goldsmith must love metal as such. A poet must love speech, must feel the glory of words, even before the thought they are to incarnate is consciously present in his brain. And he must have a peculiar perception of the beauty and power of some given literary genus—epic, tragedy, comedy, lyric. He must regard the form as something capable of a definite perfection. . . . No artist can accept progress εἰς ἄπειρον. Beyond a single thing organically complete, which he sees or foresees, there lies not progress, but dissolution; the dissolution is the formative beginning of something else.'

The doctrine of Forms, or of Literary Kinds, which in its most general shape he first derived from Brunetière, coloured much of his criticism, and perhaps the most consistently valuable part of it. He saw with more curiosity and insight than most scholars possess just what the process was. The unrivalled Greek inventiveness had left scarcely a literary form undiscovered; as Aristotle says of Democritus, they 'had thought of everything'; so that artistic progress and development became ultimately possible only by blending, by *contaminatio*, 'the horror of pedants'. Strands were now twisted; forms were crossed. There was a good case, he held, for arguing that *contaminatio*, which the nineteenth century used as the stick to beat Terence with, and Virgil, is, in fact, the very principle of literary progress, of the continuity of literature between age and age: Virgil, in flat disproof of the

Victorian doctrine that all Latin literature is second-hand, emerges as an inventive artist with, among other things, almost a new form to his credit, that of Pastoral Allegory. Mr. Phillimore's paper of 1925, *Pastoral and Allegory*, in which this is set out, I should select as perhaps the most attractive example of his literary criticism, just as I should choose his *Philostratus* essays as probably, within the classical field, his best single piece of critical scholarship. As for the astonishing translation which these essays introduce, of Philostratus's Apollonius of Tyana—that first-century mage or quack, that picturesque 'bone-setter in religion'—I can only record my conviction that had it appeared in the seventeenth or eighteenth century, in an age, that is to say, less hurried and jostled than our own, it would by now be an accepted part of English literature.

These performances lie in the route of Mr. Phillimore's profession. But there was another adventure, a study of Sir Thomas More, which could hardly have been expected from him, and for insight and divining power must take precedence of all his other critical work. You cannot be unaware that for some ten years or more now a concerted and successful effort has been made, under the enthusiastic and learned guidance of Professor R. W. Chambers, to reinstate Sir Thomas More in the high place which he deserved, and long occupied, not only in our religious and political history but in the story of English humanism and, as a master of English prose, in the history of English literature. These were questions in which Mr. Phillimore had long been interested, and for a number of years Rastell's double-column black-letter Folio of 1557 was seldom far from his hand. He thought it a scandal, as indeed it was, that this should be the only, I will not say accessible, but even extant collection of More's English works, and as early as 1905 was in correspondence with Monsieur Joseph Delcourt about the possibility of a new edition.[1] Later, with more success, he urged this duty on More's subsequent editor, Mr. W. E. Campbell.

Meanwhile, Mr. Phillimore had published in the *Dublin Review* (July 1913) the paper of which I speak,[2] its main thesis being 'that the humanist movement in England was arrested at the middle of the sixteenth century and did not mature till more than a century later; that the movement was typically personified in More; and that his death was a blow which paralysed it'. I cannot now do more than emphasize the pioneering brilliance of an essay which established the main positions of this campaign some ten or fifteen years before it had been organized. The essay, unfortunately, outside the circles of his faith, seems to have attracted little notice. Professor Chambers himself first read it as late as 1928, and I am permitted to quote, from a letter to Mr. Campbell, his first impression of it:

'I have read with very great interest the article you sent me on "The arrest of Humanism in England". I thought I had found out a number of things; but I find that J. S. Phillimore has been before me. He was a very great man. I have come to exactly the same conclusions as he on a different line of approach, as the particular authors we happened to be studying were different, I being as ignorant of the Douai and Rheims Bible as he of the Harpsfield and Rastell, though without his excuse.'

Since that date Professor Chambers has developed and matured his own prolonged researches, which may now be found in their final form in his masterly and illuminating *Life of Sir Thomas More*, published two years ago. He would not now, I believe, go quite so far as Mr. Phillimore in some directions; but the debt which he and his collaborators owe to this, as they truly call it, 'vital essay', is not sensibly diminished.

[1] In 1914, M. Delcourt published his *Essai sur la langue de Sir Thomas More d'après ses œuvres anglaises.*
[2] *Blessed Thomas More and the arrest of humanism in England.*

No portrait of Mr. Phillimore would be either true or complete which omitted his—what shall I call it?—his anti-Teutonism. By temperament and training he was of the tradition of Latin Europe, and was not readily to be persuaded that the scholars of Germany could be trusted to do much more than amass material. As coral insects they had his respect. This view he formed early, and it only strengthened with time. Even in 1899, in his Inaugural at Glasgow, I find him congratulating his new students on their national affinity to the Latin countries of Europe 'where classical culture is a birthright and not a thing of acquisition'. Three years later he was maintaining that the superiority of such a living tradition to all the industry of studious barbarism is sufficiently proved by merely observing the different sympathy and finesse with which an Italian or a Frenchman handles a classical matter—Fraccaroli or Croiset compared even with a Wilamowitz-Moellendorff. Burne-Jones once declared, of the Pergamum sculptures now at Berlin: 'Truth is, and it is a scientific induction, that whenever Germans go forth and dig, and discover, their special providence provides for them and brings to the surface the most depressing, heavy, conceited, dull products of dead-and-done-with Greece; and they ought to be thankful, for it is what they like.'

Mr. Phillimore would have liked that sentence. I think that he was sometimes too bitter about the Germans, though he had provocation enough in the degrading subservience of our scholars to Germany in the years before the last War. What inflamed him about Teutonic scholarship was its systematic fatuity, its incredulity of tradition and credulity of hypothesis. There is a kind of scholarship, also, which (if I may borrow a Johnsonian phrase) is neither content with truth nor capable of giving dignity to falsehood: all minute-hand, never telling the hour; and it cannot be denied that this species flourished in Germany. Mr. Housman, writing in 1919 to thank Mr. Phillimore for a present of one of his papers in which these resentments and others were fully and pithily expressed, wrote as follows:

'I am very much in your debt for the gift of your address, and I am glad that I did not miss it by not hearing it delivered. It contains a great deal of wholesome truth well and tellingly said, together with some things which I do not assent to. Your strictures on German scholarship have something of the intemperate zeal of the convert, like attacks on the Church of Rome by runaway monks. I should say that for the last 100 years individual German scholars have been superior in genius and intelligence as well as learning to all scholars outside Germany except Madvig and Cobet and perhaps Weil; and that the herd or group vices of the German school which you particularly reprehend took their rise from Sedan and may be expected to decline after this second and greater Jena: though indeed they have already been declining since the early years of the century. . . .'

Mr. Housman is crisp as usual, and makes his point. But he does not, you will observe, deny the vices of the herd: he only says the herd has grown smaller, and, if all goes well, will grow smaller still.

Mr. Phillimore's second volume of verses—the last he collected—appeared in 1918, and had an altogether different reception from the first. Reviewers still spoke of 'a curbed Pegasus', but the power and beauty of some of the poems was unmistakable even by men in haste. The finest group in the volume is the section of Sonnets of the Hampshire Roadside in Peace and War (though even here he must experiment—fortunately with no harm done—the lines being elongated from tens to twelves). *The Gipsies*, Ἐνόδιον Σύμβολον, *The Last Days*, *The Field of the Batteries* are poems which only accident can have kept from public knowledge and admiration. There is, besides, the noble version of Pandolfo Collenuccio's *Ode to Death*, only excelled in

swell and grandeur by the supreme poem of the book,
his *In Memoriam to Charles Fisher.*

No Charles to stride the flags in Wolsey's Quad!
    The peak has lost its eagle. Thus the veldt
Yearns lionless where late the lion trod;
    Thus yearn, when rocks in the earthquake-furnace melt,
The maimed horizons; thus the skies, if God
    Had blotted out Orion's sword and belt,
        And no gigantic huntsman, passing bold and bright,
        With starry gesture overawed the winter's night.

Daily the field of death is reaped and sown
    By land or sea; and yet no times for tears.
The zenith burns with rays of victory thrown
    Against the orient mountain-tops. What ear's
Attuned for lamentation? With no moan
    Salute the friend of six and twenty years;
        Be it uttered with Simonidean calm and pride:
        God rest his soul. Well done, and not untimely died.

Life's all a fragment. No less grandly shows
    A shattered vault, abrupt against the sky.
With ivy chevelured and the wild red rose,
    A promontory of brick, whereunder lie
Shepherd and sheep in afternoon repose
    (O'erhead, like rapier strokes the merlins fly)
        —Than undefeated frames of arch on arch that still
        Shoulder the Roman sluice intact from hill to hill.

Scraping the sands of peace, could such as he
    Get gold in block to express his character?
Had Charles not more to give and more to be
    Than aught his country had let him show for her?
Until he found his Fret-no-more at sea
    And challenged all the seas for sepulchre,
        Grew all his height, gave loose to his long-imprisoned
            power,
        And died as liked him best in the manner and in the hour.

His eye was clear and quick like streams in France.
What frank and trenchant stroke, what true mind's health,
What mirth, what scorn was his, what nonchalance
Of the ape and parrot way! No brag; no stealth;
But quintessential grace that, subtle as chance,
Makes by consent a chief-in-commonwealth:
So captainlike he rose, sans effort, from the rout;
With such Apolline shafts he rooted reptiles out.

Many whose faith implicit, doubting not
The nation's cause, said *Here am I*, soon found
A holier issue waging than they thought,
An enemy thrice the swine and thrice the hound
That Froissart dubbed him; and I know not what
Of the old good blood within their veins abound,
Calling, as deep to deep, for mates (nor far to seek)—
Good mates to die with, having God's revenge to wreak.

But who so nicely as Charles the quarrel knew?
He saw the many million hoofs, well drilled,
The tusks long-whetted, break the fences through
And run to spoil the towns of those who build
In word or stone, who reason, who still renew
By ne'er so strange reliefs, divinely willed,
The ageless guard that Rome entrusted them to mount
Over the sacred garden and the mystic fount.

He saw the self-adoring brute bedecked
(So master's weeds equip the drunken ape)
Mock-civil wise, to dupe the uncircumspect
Till the day came for German souls to escape
From feigning human, and—at large—reject
Christ for the old German God whose law is rape,
Ruin, oppression, murder, poison, sacrilege;
To whom both Turk and Hun their kindred morals pledge.

. . . .

Full oft on pilgrim feet with eyes devout
For beauty of earth and sky, or beauty in snare
Of colour seized, or forth from stone let out,
In quest of the Ancient Mother he drew that air

For which we pine who guard this last redoubt
. Of the Roman fortress: could he be unaware
        What savaging of all things courteous, fair and fine,
        Was dreamed in devildoms behind the Gallic Rhine?

And since at the European feast where purse
    Nor pedigree commends the unchartered guest,
But worser wits must, as they will, fare worse,
    None carved and broached with fuller right and zest—
Strong meats of prose and rare old wines of verse,
    With all the ironic Western muse finessed—
        Should he, grown lycanthropic-minded, fall to chew
        Weeds that some pale-eyed seer in his Bedlam garden grew?

'He's happy in whom when leaf and flower do thrive
    The idle mood of foison shall not scatter
The essential balms of honour, which survive
    When all is spent of the frail remaining matter.
These lift us out from earth and keep alive
    The former self to await and hail the latter:
        Poets in vain with meditated means of art
        Labour the vessel, once the fine perfume depart.'

Lest from the swallowing-gulfs of aftertime
    His all too frugal, too fastidious pen
Prove no alert remembrancer to climb
    And plant his name assured in History's ken,
This hedgerow garland, mine untutored rhyme,
    Shall hang and testify to Christ Church men
        That never, of all his nurslings, yet was Great Tom tolled
        For one more manly modelled and more princely souled.

Dear and familiar stones and greens, when once more peace
    Lies large on summer nights in Wolsey's moonlit Quad,
When ebb comes home to flood, in the hour when eyes release
    The arrested tear, in the hour of the reblossoming rod—
Let not the stature of his renown admit decrease,
    Who asked of seas a wave when earth denied a sod,
        And in the entombed *Invincible* for coffin laid
        As noble bones as any who fought this Last Crusade.

I cannot believe that either in Christ Church or in
Oxford such lines will ever be forgotten.

Monsignor Canon Forbes, who knew Mr. Phillimore well, has applied to him what he himself had said of Cardinal Newman:

'He was master of a tremendous team of natural faculties, and he never let go the reins; the very sense of his talents seemed to make him almost painfully cautious and exact.'

There is great truth in this, and it explains among other things some of the difficulty of his poetry. There, however, I cannot help suspecting that something more youthful and less august—I will not call it perversity— has its share of responsibility. I cannot forget that what most attracted him to the Dolomites was the pleasure of making difficult what might be easy. 'I confess', he writes somewhere, 'I know no kind of climb so fascinating and complete as to spend 11 hours on a really stiff face when there is a 'right side' to the mountain which you can trot down conveniently in 4.'

Less than three years before his death he celebrated, at the age of 51, his semi-jubilee as a Professor. I had the honour on that occasion of presenting him with his portrait, in the name of his colleagues and students and many other friends. We were met, we told him, to celebrate the scholar who had never, since we had known him, divorced literature from learning or learning from literature; for whom that unnatural modern division did not exist; whose own learning, though solid and high-built, had always been, as our ancestors would have said, polite. It was our pleasure, also, to proclaim (having him there in our power) the don who had never done or said a donnish thing; the Professor in whose company the sour face of pedantry had never been seen; the scholar and *savant* who had kept the undamaged use of all his senses, an eye for colour and light and form, and an ear for all the beauties of sound; who was a poet, and a poet of great excellence, in his own language, while he interpreted with the subtlest discernment the poets of other lands. His reply was a witty but very moving *apologia* for the life of a modern academic scholar, for time steadily withdrawn from the pursuit of literary fame and with increasing deliberation (he refused to call it self-sacrifice) devoted to the service of others: first, to his students, for whom his best could never be too good; next, to the University and City in which he lived; and after that, to the cause of *humanitas* everywhere. It has been my duty, as one of his literary executors, to examine his papers. There are many things among them that I hope may one day be collected and published, both poetry and prose. There are more that must lie, I fear, as he left them, the remains of great projects not abandoned, indeed, but subordinated to public duty.

PRINTED IN
GREAT BRITAIN
AT THE
UNIVERSITY PRESS
OXFORD
BY
JOHN JOHNSON
PRINTER
TO THE
UNIVERSITY